D1648979

Debts

and

Deficits

Hans F. Sennholz

Libertarian Press, Inc.

Spring Mills, PA 16875
(814) 422-8001

ISBN 0-910884-18-8

MANUFACTURED IN THE UNITED STATES OF AMERICA

Debts

and

Deficits

CONTENTS

Part One

Social Goals And Federal Outlays

Part II

In Search of a Solution

ACKNOWLEDGMENTS

Permission has been granted by The Foundation for Economic Education in Irvington-on-Hudson, NY, to include the essays first published in *The Freeman*, and by the *Conservative Digest* in Fort Collins, CO, to publish anew the essay, "Worse Than 1929."

The author gratefully acknowledges the help of his colleagues at the Foundation, in particular, Robert G. Anderson, Paul L. Poirot, Edmund A. Opitz, and Bettina Bien Greaves, who have read various chapters and made helpful suggestions. He is indebted to the Grove City College librarian, Diane H. Grundy-McKillop, who patiently assisted in assembling and checking facts and figures. His thanks are justly due to his son and daughter-in-law, Robert and Lyn, who, as publishers are laboring diligently on the production and distribution of his work. The author also gratefully acknowledges the help of his wife and partner in life.

INTRODUCTION

The man who lives above his present circumstances is in great danger of soon living much beneath them. The same is true with a group of people called "society." To live beyond its means is to invite poverty and deprivation in the end. As prodigality may cause a person to fall into poverty, misery and even disgrace, so does deficit spending minister to all sorts of political evil. It consumes substance and wealth, engages in mass deceit about economic reality, sets a poor example to others, makes people dependent and subservient, causes uncertainty and instability, and breeds social conflict and strife. It may even weaken the political institutions of a free society.

Every day, we either improve our material well-being through saving, or reduce it through overconsumption. Businessmen either form capital through reinvestment of their earnings, or dissipate it through losses or overconsumption. Every day, economic conditions in the United States either improve or deteriorate, the levels of living either rise or fall, depending on our consumption habits relative to our means and circumstances. In short, our economic future is greatly affected by the difference between our income and expenditures.

Most people are reluctant to apply this basic principle of economic well-being to their governments. Surely, they are aware of it in their own financial affairs; however, political organizations are believed to be endowed with mysterious powers surpassing or negating this economic principle. The belief in such powers derives strength and support from the material benefits which many people gain from government and its redistributive programs. Their immediate gain may outweigh the vague fear of societal losses in the future.

From their very beginning, the redistribution policies of the U.S. government have consumed productive capital on a massive scale. At first, they merely slowed down capital accumulation and production improvement. With the acceleration of government spending in recent years, further accumulation of capital was finally checked. In fact, a convincing case can be made that the United States has embarked upon net consumption of capital that was accumulated in the past. Our capital-intensive industries, such as the manufacture of automobiles, steel, pharmaceutical products, tools and dies, etc., find it increasingly difficult to compete with foreign industries even in domestic markets. Capital-intensive industries are universally depressed, setting capital and labor free for employment in less intensive industries. That is, labor is moving from industries with high rates of capital investment to less productive employment. According to our estimates, purchasing power income of American workers actually has declined some 15% since 1977.

When the public demand for government services and benefits grows beyond the ability of business and wealthy taxpayers to pay, budgetary deficits become unavoidable. After all, the popularity of redistribution by political force tends to grow with every dollar of "free" service rendered. The clamor finally becomes so intense that, in order to be heard, every new call is presented as an "emergency" that must be met immediately before all others. Redistributive government then rushes from one emergency to another, trying to meet the most noisy and politically potent demands. As no one wants to pay for the new expenditures, least of all the beneficiaries, the transfer administration is bound to suffer budgetary deficits.

When a corporation suffers losses for long periods of time, it inevitably comes to the end of its capital substance, at which time it ceases to operate. Whatever assets are left will be distributed to its creditors. While government deficits may not soon lead to bankruptcy, they nevertheless have identical economic consequences. They destroy productive capital. Indeed, the deficits of the U.S. government have consumed, and continue to consume, capital substance on a scale far greater than all losing enterprises combined. During the 1950s, total U.S. government deficits amounted to a mere $17.7 billion. During the 1960s, they rose to $56.9 billion. Deficits during the 1970s soared to $365 billion and, as if they were following an exponential curve, to $673 billion during the first half of the 1980s and an estimated $1 trillion during the second half.

It is difficult to estimate the number of factories and stores that were not built, the tools and dies that were not cast, the jobs not created, the wages not paid, the food, clothing and shelter not produced on account of this massive consumption of capital. The coming generation of Americans and countless others to come will be poorer by far as a result of our deficit spending.

Of course, the beneficiaries of the redistribution process may enjoy every moment of it. With present-oriented people, today's enjoyment is always more pleasurable than saving for tomorrow. In their ignorance, they may applaud the very favors and handouts that are destroying their jobs and the wages they could have earned. Costly emergency programs may be hailed as progress while they actually check economic progress. The bank or insurance company that is investing the people's savings in Treasury bonds, notes, or bills may be enjoying "safety" for its investments. The fact is that it is channeling potentially productive savings into the maelstrom of government consumption. The returns it seeks from its investments will not come from new production, but from taxes that need to be collected in the future.

In dim awareness of the importance of capital, some social spenders are quick to maintain that government spending is merely another form of investing. They want government to "invest" in a greater society that is to be built by political force and economic redistribution. Their judgment of what is most urgent and important is to prevail for all others.

No matter what the objective of the spending program may be, government expenditures always constitute economic costs that are borne by taxpayers, lenders, or inflation victims. Even where government builds roads or canals, federal buildings or airports, the expenditures usually cannot pass the tests of the market. Demanded by voters, built by politicians, and administered by bureaucrats, public works constitute huge malinvestments that waste scarce resources and consume productive capital. In fact, they waste funds faster than most other spending programs.

As economic improvements may accelerate through ever higher rates of saving and investing, so may conditions deteriorate through accelerating capital consumption. No matter what our incomes may be, if we consume more than we produce, we are eating into our productive substance. Once we consume capital, while stubbornly clinging to accustomed levels of consumption, we descend at ever faster rates. The stockholder who liquidates some stock to boost his living expenditures faces lower income in the future. If, thereafter, he maintains his level of living, he will have to liquidate his holdings faster and faster until the last share is sold. Obviously, he could halt his impoverishment at any time, or restore his fortune, through appropriate curtailment of his living expenses.

For a future-oriented, determined individual it may be relatively easy to readjust his consumption to falling income. For a society consisting of millions of voters who are bent on redistribution and consumption through the political apparatus, this readjustment may be rather difficult. Given the public ignorance about the significance of productive capital, the political pressures for government benefits and services may grow when incomes are falling. The very forces that are debilitating productive capital through overconsumption are likely to oppose any reduction in consumption. They may move heaven and earth to maintain their spending levels which, after all, come from "social benefits and services" to which they believe they are morally and politically entitled. Thus, the process of dissipation, once begun, feeds on the public pressures for simple preservation of the economic way of life to which we have grown accustomed.

If declining productivity and incomes should finally cut into transfer benefits and services, the beneficiaries may rise in anger about the sudden "violation of their rights." There may be social disturbance and disruption of the production process, which would reduce output and income even further, which in turn would further aggravate the situation. A vicious circle of frustration and decline!

Even without this particular force of acceleration, we may consume productive capital at accelerating rates. Many people react to declining real incomes from employment by producing less. They may even blame their employers, those "greedy" and "ruthless" corporations, whom the demagogues will be quick to condemn for the decline. Absenteeism, slowdowns, work stoppages, featherbedding, and other restrictive work practices may grow worse. Lower output because of lower labor efficiency raises labor costs and dissipates productive capital.

To arrest and reverse this dissipation of our productive substance is the greatest economic challenge of our time. We must learn anew to live within our means. Government on all levels must balance its budgets and refrain from consuming productive capital. For a representative government, such as ours, to practice economy and frugality, the electorate must first be convinced of the desirability of such old-fashioned virtues. Public opinion, or public sentiment, which is able to sustain or change any policy, must point the way.

For all the noise about the federal deficits, unfortunately there is no indication that the American public and its representatives in the Congress are serious about the need for balanced budgets. Public pressure for redistribution benefits causes committee after committee to vote itself and its constituents huge increases in funding. The Senate Banking Committee is considering a $10 billion increase over the President's budget request, which already envisions a huge deficit. The Senate Labor and Human Resources Committee is debating an $8 billion overrun. The spokesmen of American agriculture are demanding another boost in farm price supports. The old pressure groups and their big spenders in Congress continue on their merry way.

The deficit hypocrisy that is stalking the halls of Congress is filling us with deep pessimism about our economic, social and political future. If we cannot return to fiscal integrity because the public prefers profusion and prodigality over balanced budgets, we cannot escape paying the price, which is ever lower incomes and standards of living for all. The pains of economic stagnation and decline which are plaguing us today are likely to intensify and multiply in the coming years. The social and racial conflict, which springs from the redistribution ideology, may deepen as economic output is shrinking and transfer "entitlements" cause budget deficits to soar. The U.S. dollar, which has become a mere corollary of government finance, is unlikely to survive the soaring deficits.

We do not know whether our republic will survive this century. If it is to survive, we must overcome all transfer temptations. We must reverse the trend and reduce the role of government in our lives. With religious fervor and unbounded courage, we must resist all transfer temptations, no matter what our legal entitlement may be. No matter how the transfer system has victimized us in the past, we must not accept a penny of transfer payment. To effect a rebirth of the free society, we must cease and desist from preying on each other through the apparatus of politics.

PART ONE

Social Goals
and
Federal Outlays

1

THE POLITICS OF DEFICIT SPENDING

The Federal Budget

A budget may be described as an itemized summary of probable receipts and expenditures for a given period. As such, it is also a plan of action, defining goals and outlining expectations. Budgeting is the art of living within the constraints of the budget.

The federal budget is a financial plan that relates prospective expenditures by federal agencies to expected revenues over a fiscal year. Like a family budget, or that of a social club or business enterprise, the federal budget is a financial program that provides pertinent information about goals and activities. It is by far the largest of all budgets, affecting the economic lives of every individual in the United States. It is characterized by a great complexity that is growing with its size.

During the first 150 years of U.S. history, it was a maxim of political economy that the federal government should balance its budget. Honesty and integrity demanded of all political parties and administrations that they balance the budget. The only exception to the rule was allowed in wartime, when deficits were deemed to be unavoidable. When the war emergency had passed, the federal government was expected to repay the debt as soon as possible. It was made to run surpluses for 28 consecutive years after the Civil War, and for 11 consecutive years after World War I.

The debacle of the Great Depression, together with the sway of Keynesian economics, gave rise to a new belief that, in periods of economic decline and stagnation, budgetary deficits could serve to stimulate economic activity. The deficits were supposed to be offset by surpluses in periods of prosperity so that the budget would remain in balance over the business cycle as a whole. As was to be expected, the "contracyclical budget" did not bring about stability and did not remain in balance. Instead, it invited politicians and government officials to engage in wasteful and self-serving expenditures. It not only sanctioned executive and bureaucratic profligacy, but also encouraged congressional "pork-barreling." In short, it bred huge budgetary deficits not only during recessions, but also at other times.

Since the coming of the Great Society, even the Keynesian modicum of fiscal discipline has gradually slipped away. Budgets still are viewed as contracyclical tools, but primarily are used as free-for-all for special interests. In boom and recession, the federal government now suffers substantial deficits. In fact, in 24 of the last 25 years, it incurred deficits that grew larger nearly every year—exceeding 2.5 percent of gross national product in all but one of the past ten years and averaging over 5 percent in the last three years. Fourteen cents of every dollar spent by the federal government now come from lenders rather than taxpayers.

The growing deficits have left a mountain of federal debt. By the end of World War II, it had soared to some $245 billion and 133 percent of gross national product. Although a substantial further increase in dollar debt occurred between 1946 and 1971, the ratio of debt to GNP fell sharply, and by 1971 had fallen to prewar levels. Most of this was the result of inflation, which accelerated the rise of GNP in monetary terms and depreciated the debt. By 1981, the federal debt exceeded the one trillion dollar mark and amounted to 33.6 percent of GNP. In 1986, it climbed above the 2 trillion mark and some 50.4 percent of GNP.[1] At the present rate of deficit spending, it will reach 3 trillion dollars and surpass 60 percent of GNP before the end of the decade.

Ambivalent Voters

The record of deficit spending by the federal government depresses and frightens most Americans. They worry that they are living on borrowed time that some day must end, or in a dream world that will crash like the stock market did in 1929. They sense that something is wrong and that, in the end, the federal debt will hurt their own financial situation. After all, debts need to be paid, even government debts. Yet, this concern among voters is difficult to grasp as a tangible, solvable problem. They do not see the deficit as an immediate threat, nor do they perceive a crisis that needs to be solved today. Therefore, they are unwilling to take the painful steps that are believed to be essential to reduce the deficit drastically.

The American people overwhelmingly support reductions in federal spending, but they balk at virtually every proposal of specific cuts. A nationwide poll conducted by the *Wall Street Journal* and NBC News, for instance, found that many Americans express alarm about the federal deficit, but resist any attempt at reducing federal spending. The poll found that 86 percent oppose reductions in Medicare benefits, which the President had proposed in his budget message. Sixty-nine percent oppose spending reductions on social programs for the poor. Half oppose the President's elimination of federal subsidies to local mass-transit systems. They also oppose proposals to boost federal taxation. Some 56 percent oppose income tax boosts.[2]

Many Americans deny that, at the present, the deficit has a direct impact on their lives; but they are convinced that spending cuts and higher taxes would. The latter are real, but the value of balancing the budget is very abstract. Spending cuts could adversely affect some 90 million Americans who depend on government dollars for support. There are more than 35 million elderly who receive old-age social security, railroad, veterans, federal civil service, and state and local retirement benefits, some 9 million recipients of survivor benefits, 6 million beneficiaries of supplemental income programs, 6 million unemployed individuals and their dependents, and finally, some 2 million individuals in the armed services and more than 16 million government employees,[3] who in turn support some 20 million dependents.

Expressed in terms of federal assistance for those deemed poor and needy, the federal government, through Medicaid and Medicare, pays for the medical care of more than 50 million aged, disabled, and needy Americans. It subsidizes approximately 95 million meals per day, or 14 percent of all meals served, through a food stamp program, child nutrition program, nutrition programs for the elderly, and commodity distribution programs. It provides training for almost one million low-income disadvantaged people and pays housing assistance to some 3.4 million American households. Last but not least, it offers some 6.9 million post-secondary awards or loans to students and their parents through student assistance programs.

The indirect effects of these benefit programs reach nearly every American home. The retirement benefits to some 35 million beneficiaries lend aid and comfort to family members who otherwise would have to support the elderly. The Medicaid and Medicare programs that finance the medical care of more than 50 million aged, disabled and needy Americans lighten the financial burden not only of the aged, disabled and needy, but also of the families that otherwise would provide the medical care. The federal subsidies to some 95 million meals served every day benefit not only the individuals who enjoy the meals but also all those who provide them. The federal student assistance programs subsidize not only 6.9 million students, but also many more parents, relatives and spouses who otherwise might provide the assistance. In short, the federal deficits, so it seems, do not have a direct impact on the lives of all these people, but spending cuts and higher taxes would. The $2 trillion debt is like another galaxy trillions of light years away; but a two-dollar reduction in benefits may be felt as a glaring injustice that is opposed strenuously.

Many Americans undoubtedly would view deficit spending in a different light if its dire consequences were more clearly visible. If it were accompanied by rampant inflation or deep depression with mass unemployment, they would disapprove it immediately. Surely, they would not tolerate it as a deliberate policy if the harm it inflicts on nearly every voter, including the direct beneficiaries of the deficit largesse, were to visibly exceed the benefits of the spending. Unfortunately, the harmful consequences of deficit spending are not clearly visible in the haze of popular notions and prejudices. It takes economic knowledge and logical reasoning to perceive that deficit spending consumes economic wealth and substance and mortgages the future, that it is a potent prescription for stagnation and poverty, an open invitation to monetary inflation and depreciation, and a free-for-all for social and political conflict. Moreover, the perception tends to be clouded by the enticements of the benefit programs. Ninety million beneficiaries of spending programs are likely to question the validity of economic knowledge and the cogency of economic reasoning as long as they expect to gain from the largess.

Congressional Profligacy

To most Americans, the day of reckoning seems far off; deficit reduction may be a vaguely moral imperative that lacks financial significance. To most members of the U.S. Congress who incur the deficits and pyramid the debt, the issue is purely materialistic. Utterly unaware of any questions of the morality of deficits and debts, they are guided by political pragmatism aiming at "solving problems," especially the problem of getting re-elected and advancing their own political careers.

While serving in the U.S. Congress, Ron Paul of Texas encountered gross pragmatism building on economic fallacies and misconceptions that led his colleagues to engage in open-handed spending. Most members of Congress, he observed, are convinced that government should provide food, housing, medical care for the poor, retirement benefits for the elderly and guaranteed jobs for everyone. They believe that the private-property individual-enterprise economic order fails to deal with the people's needs, that it serves the profit interests of capitalists and entrepreneurs while it shortchanges the vital interests of working people. Guided by such notions of economic order they seek to "redistribute" income and wealth by favoring one class of people at the expense of another. They are ever mindful that such favors also yield political advantages to themselves, for the class they favor is more numerous and powerful at the polls than the class forced to bear the expense. They call this "representing the majority view of their district" and voting "the desires of the district," which is most likely to enhance their political careers, at least in the short run. What happens in the long run may be of no concern to most members of the U.S. Congress.[4]

In June 1982, President Reagan created a commission to conduct a "private sector survey on cost control" of the executive branch of the federal government. The commission, named after its chairman, New York businessman J. Peter Grace, conducted a comprehensive study of government efficiency in order to iden-

tify—and hopefully eliminate—wasteful spending in government. It soon concluded that much of the responsibility for excessive spending lies not with the Administration, but with Congress.

In a scintillating tract called *Pork Barrel*, Randall Fitzgerald
and Gerald Lipson, two of Peter Grace's associates on the Commission, tell the unexpurgated Grace Commission story.[5] In more
than one hundred examples of pork-barreling by members of the
Congress, almost evenly divided between Democrats and Repub-
licans, liberals and conservatives, the authors illustrate the appetite
for political spending. Most politicians live by a "parochial imperative" that elevates local interests over all others. In particular, it
makes the members of Congress bring new federal spending into
their districts, no matter how dubious and unnecessary it may be;
they are to secure subsidies to any and all economic interests in
their districts and prevent changes or reductions in the size of
federal spending by federal facilities at the local level; they are
to prevent competitive bidding procedures if this benefits local
interests, and bring about the cancellation of state and local
liabilities to the federal government when they become burden-
some.[6]

Most members of Congress living by the "parochial imperative"
are guided by erroneous notions and doctrines. They act under
the misconception that local interests, as they see them, coincide
with the national interest. To promote trade, commerce and industry in their district, they are convinced, is to promote economic
life in various districts. When one district is made to prosper, the
prosperity of all is enhanced. Such reasoning is rather spurious;
it ignores the fact that the favors granted in one district demand
material sacrifices from people in all districts. The entitlements
of some individuals must ultimately be matched by tax exactions
from other individuals. Parochial politicians plead the case for
"special local interest," which differs fundamentally from "local
interest properly understood." The former always necessitates government coercion to confer benefits and grant privileges to some
people and withhold them from others. The "properly understood
local interest" calls for no coercion by police, judges and tax
collectors; it actually reduces coercion and restraint and concurs
with the national interest, yea, even the international interest. It

calls for expansion of the sphere of individual freedom to satisfy human wants and sustain human life, the freedom that embodies the right to the fruits of individual effort, which is the quintessence of private property.

To justify benefits and privileges, parochial politicians argue like the talkative highwayman who lectures his victims about the benefits of more equitable distribution that is to benefit everyone, even his victims. He obviously ignores the fact that the highway principle, when practiced by everyone, would render economic production rather hazardous and, in the end, gravely jeopardize human existence.

Micromanagement

To serve the parochial imperative, legislators seek to expand the scope of their concern for administrative activities to include minute details of operations. They practice "micromanagement," which is congressional involvement in day-to-day management decisions. Congress may direct executive branch agencies to employ more labor than the agency managers say they need, to place labor in locations where they are not needed, to prevent changes in the size or location of offices and agencies. Congress may order the Veterans Administration, with more than 200,000 employees, to seek Congressional approval for any reorganization affecting as few as three employees. Individual Senators and Congressmen may obtain special legislation that takes funds from the public treasury to grant favors to this group or that faction, who in turn promise re-election.

Any administrative effort to streamline and modernize the government's organizational structures is met by persistent Congressional resistance, which keeps most operations obsolete, inefficient, and costly. Members of Congress usually intervene to thwart or delay structural reorganization. They in turn are pressured and made to block the way by government employees directly affected by reorganization. Waxing on human and financial losses which reorganization and consolidation would inflict on them, employees and their unions exert direct pressure through protest marches, letters, and telephone calls, and generate indirect pressure enlisting the support and influence of Congressional staff that often depends on them for information, advice and help.

It is the function of boards of directors of private corporations to set basic rules and policies. To set aside or waive the rules to benefit friends or associates is gross nepotism and corruption that may call for indictment and punishment. The U.S. Congress writes the rules for administrative operations, but all too often turns around and makes exceptions to the rules. Influential members of Congress usually exercise the very kind of favoritism which the rules were supposed to prevent. They write program rules, and immediately make exceptions for friends. In commerce and industry, they would face SEC investigation and indictment.

Basic principles of sound management require executives to have the authority to use labor most effectively, to assign it in the service of customers, and change assignments to meet changing business needs. In private enterprise, this authority is a basic ingredient of efficient management. In the U.S. government, Congress frequently negates this management authority to protect federal employees against the kinds of change and challenge which employees of private corporations face all the time. Many members of Congress act like union stewards whose primary concern is the convenience of their members. Moreover, in contrast to union stewards, legislators have the clout to turn their concerns into law. They may even mandate personnel requirements, eight positions for an EPA laboratory at Grosse Isle, Michigan, ten positions for wastewater treatment construction projects in Washington, D.C., five EPA positions for implementing strategies regarding the Chesapeake Bay, etc. They may prescribe personnel policies to the Department of Commerce, the Department of Justice, the Department of Education, the Department of Labor, the Department of Agriculture, the Defense Department, and other agencies and commissions.

Many members of Congress ardently oppose any administrative effort to save money by "privatizing" federal functions and services and by "contracting out" for the products and services the government needs. To save the jobs of threatened federal employees, the legislators intervene by investigating and pressuring federal managers until they surrender to the Congressional pressure.

After all, why should anyone want to privatize or contract out if he has nothing to gain personally, but invariably will suffer trouble and harrassment for his effort?

Eugene Joseph McCarthy, long-time U.S. Senator from Minnesota, explains Congressional profligacy in terms of a "double standard" of economic rationale—one standard at home, and another for the rest of the country. Members of Congress readily declare their great commitments to frugality and austerity in all matters that are of no visible account to their constituents, but unflinchingly champion the special interests in their states or districts. The local press, radio and television, even the Chamber of Commerce, and especially the member's political opponents adhere to the same double standard. They expect members of Congress to wax eloquent about frugality and then give tangible evidence of their effectiveness by having the federal government build a new post office, a government office building, a veterans' hospital, housing for the elderly, more roads, bridges, etc. Nothing reveals the double standard more clearly, according to Senator McCarthy, than a water project, a dam, lock or canal, that may be named after the politician who sponsored it. Even the most frugal fiscal conservative who says "no" to many transfer programs may readily spend billions of dollars for the illusion of immortality through enduring government projects named after him.[7]

Running a close second in Congressional popularity are military installations of every kind. They enjoy popular support on a variety of grounds: national security, national tradition and history, and regional economic impact. The Department of Defense is spending more than $20 billion a year to operate some 5,000 military installations and properties, many of which have become unnecessary, inefficient, or uneconomical. Every state and more than one-half of all Congressional districts contain or border on military bases and installations that bring generous payrolls and lucrative procurements. They yield income and wealth to the districts although the posts may be visible reminders of the Civil War, yea, even the War of 1812. They may be military anomalies, well suited for military museums, but they continue to withstand all attempts at closing them. The Congressional parochial imperative, ironclad and under arms, is repelling all assaults.

Executive Politics

Like Congress, the executive branch has its own porkbarrel projects. After all, it consists of politicians who manage to come to power by the very imperative that brings the members of Congress to Washington. Politicians in power broaden and extend the imperative to include the whole nation, which costs billions of dollars. A Congressman may deem himself efficient and successful to land a one-million dollar government contract for his friends in the district. The President of the United States, as the November election approaches, may propose federal expenditures costing tens of billions of dollars.

During the 1964 election, Lyndon B. Johnson introduced his Great Society by "declaring war on poverty" and promising to eradicate it within this century. When elected by a landslide, he built his particular pork barrel with government projects benefiting his followers. He sponsored the Economic Opportunity Act of 1964, established the Office of Economic Opportunity (OEO), and introduced many new antipoverty programs. The landmarks of his Great Society are easy to identify: the Social Security Amendments of 1965, creating health insurance programs for the aged and needy through Medicare and Medicaid; the Elementary and Secondary Education Act of 1965, which constituted the first general school aid legislation ever, targeting money to schools with poor children; the Housing and Urban Development Act of 1968, which meant to help low- and moderate-income families buy their own homes; and the Civil Rights Acts of 1964, 1965, and 1968, prohibiting racial discrimination in school, employment, housing, and public accommodation.

The executive branch deals with matters of greater sweep, costing much larger sums of money. President Johnson sought to purchase his immortality in the annals of the American republic with programs that already have cost more than one trillion dollars and will cost many more in the future. In 1972, President Nixon sought to imitate his predecessor through increases in Social Security involving many billions of dollars. It is a clear example of both the Congress and the Executive rolling the barrel back and forth and claiming full credit in the end. As the November 1972 election approached, the President recommended a 5 percent boost in Social Security benefits, which would sit well with elderly voters. Not to be outdone, the Democratic opposition demanded a 10 percent boost, which the President threatened to veto for being fiscally irresponsible. To outclass, outmaneuver and embarrass the President, Congress finally enacted a 20 percent raise and ordered it to commence immediately. Surely, the President was expected to veto a twenty percent raise, having threatened to veto any increase above 5 percent. Instead, he readily signed the ploy into law and informed all recipients, in a note accompanying Social Security checks, that he had signed the bill. Both the President and members of Congress now claimed credit for the payments.

A favorite executive strategem designed to obtain an advantage over one's political opponents is to sponsor new spending on grounds that one is merely "heading off" a Congressional move to increase the spending. The President may double and triple federal outlays for agricultural price supports, saying that he is merely heading off a Congressional move to boost the support prices even further. He may propose any transfer program and engage in any spending scheme on grounds of "heading off" his opponents. The Congress in turn may launch its porkbarrels to head off the President. As one seeks to outdo the other, both run faster and faster in the race, currying the favors of special-interest voters. As of now, both runners continue to accelerate, dispensing taxpayer money on the way; the spectators who are taxpayers are very nervous and weary; after all, the runners are buying votes with their money.

The contestants of both branches of government are running a tight race, moving in large packs, spending and politicking together, and pointing at each other for engaging in wasteful spending and dissipation of economic substance and well-being. It does not matter whether they are running in multitudes and spending in unison, the responsibility and guilt are as great and truly personal as if each alone had caused the dissipation. Capacity and power always walk hand in hand with responsibility.

Bureaucratic Management

The spendthrifts of Congress and the profligates in the Executive receive encouragement and support from an army of civil servants who actually do the spending. They are the regulars of the administrative organization, the bureaucracy which is always ready and eager to spend more money. After all, civil servants usually know how to improve and expand their operations, provided they are granted more money. The police commissioner can provide more police protection, the Internal Revenue Service can conduct more audits to collect more revenue, the city-owned transportation system can purchase more busses or subway cars, the community hospital can offer better health care services. They all can expand and improve their operations by spending more money.[8]

When individual enterprise is free and unhampered, profit-and-loss calculations set precise limits to a businessman's temptations to expand his services. Business accounting, which ascertains success or failure of an operation, reveals the desirability of capital expenditures. In particular, it discloses the return from an investment in relation to the capital outlay. When the costs of an outlay exceed its return, the businessman is forced to retrench and restrain his ambition. Failure to do so would invite losses, which would cast serious doubt on his managerial ability.

A government agency or bureau faces no such limitation. Its services, no matter how valuable they may be, have no market price and, therefore, cannot be subjected to profit-and-loss accounting. They are open-ended unless they are restrained by precise rules and regulations, that is, bureaucratic directives. Lest government agents become irresponsible spenders of the taxpayers' money, they need detailed instructions about every aspect of their operations. Thus, forever restrained by rules and regulations, they are anxiously pleading for more authority and more money. They are the regulars of government largess and the natural allies of all would-be spenders in the Congress and the Executive. They serve ideally as motivated expert witnesses and spokesmen for any and all causes their allies care to invoke.

The same is true with civil servants managing enterprises owned and operated by the federal, state or local government in a country with a preponderant enterprise system. Such "public enterprises" can be subjected to profit-and-loss accounting. Yet, it must be remembered that they are made "public" precisely because government wants to deviate from the profit system. Government "nationalizes," "socializes," or launches an enterprise because it does not want production or service for the greatest possible profit. It pursues other tasks and objectives that are deemed "more important," "more urgent," "higher," etc. In every case, it wants to favor some people at the expense of others.

A city-owned transportation system may charge its customers a fare that does not cover the cost of operation; it may grant preferential rates to certain commuters in certain locations, or it may pay its unionized workers exceptionally high wages and expensive fringe benefits for minimal labor exertion. All such objectives usually cause operating losses that must be borne by taxpayers.

The losses of public enterprises are not considered a proof of failure. The civil servant who manages the city-owned bus authority is not responsible for the loss; he merely follows the regulations and serves the "more important," "more urgent," "higher" objectives. He is a faithful servant of these objectives, defending the goals and explaining the deficits, and arguing for larger appropriations. After all, an able civil servant always knows how he can expand the service of his public enterprise and how to serve ever "higher objectives" provided the required funds are made available. His position and function make him an important ally of the champions of similar objectives in the Congress and the Executive.

The federal budget is permeated by the notions and doctrines of "higher objectives." In workaday, prosaic terminology, it seeks to favor some people at the expense of others. It is a plan of action estimating the costs of political transfer, and a public declaration proclaiming the politics of deficit spending. As such, it reveals much of the theory and practice of public morality.

2

INCOME BY MAJORITY VOTE

The Rationale

Throughout the ages, philosophers inquiring into the nature of things rarely reflected upon the individual. Their primary focal point was on humanity as a whole, or the nation, city state, class, or race. They searched for the past of their collective whole or the end toward which it was supposed to lead. The individual was expected to adjust his actions to the collective destiny as envisioned by the philosophers. Failure to adjust invited moral censure and condemnation.

Most philosophers were bent on reforming and reconstructing society. They looked upon mankind from the throne of a benevolent king or prince, or from the platform of an omnipotent state which, in their judgment, could organize society as it pleased. Utterly unaware of any regularity and invariance of human action, of the laws and principles of social cooperation by which man must live to attain his chosen objectives, they fervently invoked political power to usher in their utopias. In one way or another they favored authoritarianism and despotism.

The discovery of inexorable principles of human action by French Physiocrats and British political economists during the eighteenth century gave birth to a new view of society. Instead of judging human phenomena by arbitrary philosophical standards, economists began to study the eternal laws of human action and social cooperation. The French Physiocrats from François Quesnay (1694–1774) to Anne Robert Jacques Turgot (1727–1781) and Pierre Samuel Du Pont de Nemours (1739–1817) and the great classical economists from Adam Smith (1723–1790) to Jean Baptiste Say (1767–1832), David Ricardo (1772–1823), and Nassau

William Senior (1790–1864) discovered many regularities of market phenomena. Unfortunately, they did not extricate themselves completely from the shackles of ancient thought. They remained enmeshed in some holistic concepts, such as factor income and wealth. Their focal point was on the distribution of income to factors of production: land, labor and capital. They distinguished between agricultural proprietors earning rents, commercial and industrial entrepreneurs earning profits, and laborers earning wages. The distribution of income, in turn, was seen as an important indicator of the relative position of different groups of society.

The last of the classical economists, John Stuart Mill (1806–1873), whose *Principles of Political Economy* went through seven editions in his lifetime, making him the leading economic authority throughout most of the second half of the nineteenth century, unfortunately returned to the ancient view of income and wealth. He cast out some inexorable principles of income allocation and concluded that individual income may be the product of human institutions and, therefore, be arbitrary. In his own words, "Unlike the laws of Production, those of Distribution are partly of human institution: since the manner in which wealth is distributed in any given society, depends on the statutes or usages therein obtaining. But though governments or nations have the power of deciding what institutions shall exist, they cannot arbitrarily determine how those institutions shall work. The conditions on which the power they possess over the distribution of wealth is dependent, and the manner in which the distribution is effected by the various modes of conduct which society may think fit to adopt, are as much a subject for scientific inquiry as any of the physical laws of nature."[1]

John Stuart Mill and his many disciples probably paved the way for Karl Marx (1818–1883) who was to set the tone for most income discussion after Mill. During the twentieth century, the Marxian body of thought was to become the most important source from which labor legislation throughout the world draws its intellectual support. Marx built on Mill's "institutional" distribution of income and concluded that the institution of private property in the means of production invariably and mercilessly leads to exploitation of workers by capitalists. Only labor creates value, and since laborers do not receive all the proceeds of production, they are exploited. The exploitation in turn is bound to culminate in violent revolution and the establishment of proletarian dictatorships.

Profit-seeking capitalists exploit their workers by forcing them to work without remuneration and create "surplus value." In Marx's own words: "Like every other increase in the productiveness of labor, machinery is intended to cheapen commodities, and, by shortening that portion of the workingday, in which the labourer works for himself, to lengthen the other portion that he gives, without an equivalent, to the capitalist. In short, it is a means for producing surplus value."[2]

All over the world, the exploitation theory has become a universal guidepost for labor legislation and regulation. In the United States, it is visible in the eagerness of both political parties to provide protection to working people from the discretion and power of corporations, and allocate income by majority vote. The individual worker is believed to be helpless and in need of protection from management, whose primary concerns are said to be power and profit. The unbridled market order with its profit motive and unhampered competition stands condemned for inflicting cruel hardship on helpless victims. All such notions, which are popular versions of the exploitation theory, are taught at all colleges and universities, are enunciated by nearly all textbooks, proclaimed by all channels of communication, elaborated by vocal labor leaders, and acted upon by legislators at all levels of government.

The growing mountain of labor legislation, which is the pride of all "progressive" countries, is the fruit of the exploitation doctrine. Compulsory social insurance, including Medicare and Medicaid, is the most expensive fruit. The private property order is said to be incapable of giving sustenance and dignity to the unemployed, sick, and elderly workers; therefore, social policy must fill the gap and assure decent living conditions to an ever-larger part of the population. Its advocates credit governments and labor unions for having reduced the work week from more than 60 hours a week to 40 hours, and eliminated women's and children's labor. They applaud politicians for setting minimum wage rates and mandating fringe benefits, and hail union officials for having improved the workers' lot.

Entitlements for Seniors

The primary task of most politicians today is to provide, and then guide, their constituents to the government benefit and entitlement troughs. They readily defend the troughs and loudly cheer the imbibers. Many champion the cause of senior citizens who, in American political life, are first in line.

While the elderly comprise about 11 to 12 percent of the total U.S. population, they receive some 30 percent of federal budget outlays and more than 40 percent of federal tax revenues. Their shares are scheduled to rise in the coming years, as federal spending for the elderly is rising considerably faster than overall federal spending. The Old Age Survivors and Disability Insurance programs now provide monthly cash payments to some 26 million people who are 62 or older. Compensation payments to service-connected disabled veterans and pensions for aged veterans benefit over 2 million aged veterans and survivors. Medicare, Medicaid, and other health programs provide benefits to some 99 percent of the aged population. Rent subsidies and loan interest subsidies are granted to 2.25 million elderly households through HUD subsidized housing programs. Service centers and meals-on-wheels serve some 600,000 meals per day to the elderly. Older American Act programs provide community services and assistance to low-income elderly in meeting high energy costs. Finally, state and local government outlays on public welfare and health care contribute to what officials like to call "the income security of aged Americans."

The cornerstone of this massive transfer of income and wealth from taxpayers to aged beneficiaries is the Social Security System. No matter what we may think of the motive powers that gave birth to the System, we cannot deny that it is the greatest political transfer system ever devised. In 1986, it was estimated that the United States Social Security System paid $203.8 billion to some 23 million retired workers, 3.1 million disabled workers and their 14.9 million dependents and survivors. One hundred twenty-six million workers and their employers paid an estimated $201.5 billion in payroll taxes to cover these costs.[3]

Ironically, in most of its endeavors, the transfer state accomplishes the very opposite of what it sets out to achieve. The

Social Security System, with all its political intentions, is probably the most spectacular failure of them all. As a scheme designed to alleviate unemployment, it has failed dismally. It was supposed to retire older workers to open up more jobs for younger workers. Unfortunately, the unemployment problem it was intended to solve is still with us, with all its urgency and severity. Millions of Americans walking the streets in idleness and dejection are testimony to that fact, although Social Security benefits are now received by nearly all senior Americans and, if disability payments are included, by one in every six Americans.

The System was intended to endow every person with the right to a minimum income upon retirement, lest he should become dependent upon his family and others. Unfortunately, it has weakened the will to independence, and has subjected most retirees to dependence upon the discretion and benevolence of politicians.

Politicians determine the conditions of eligibility. They define the concepts of "covered employment," retirement age, limits of earned income, the tax rates on covered workers and employers, ceilings on taxable wages, etc. They define the rights of a covered worker's dependents to additional benefits. In other words, there is not a single phase of our Social Security program that does not depend on the politicians' notions of social justice and economic adequacy.

Though the promise of Social Security to create full employment has turned out to be a false one, and though Social Security recipients are now dependent upon the impersonal welfare state for sustenance, still, Social Security seems to have wide-spread support. Why is Social Security favored by so many?

The most common argument is based on error and wishful thinking. Social Security recipients are convinced that they actually earned their benefits. "I paid in, I contributed," they answer in unison. Such a statement discloses probably the most common misconception about Social Security. Most recipients apparently believe that they are drawing out in benefits what they contributed in the past. In reality, the connection between benefits received and payments contributed is rather weak.

Simple calculation easily ascertains that many present beneficiaries withdraw in several months what they contributed since the initiation of the system. After they have received the equivalent of their own contributions, the "right" to old-age income obviously constitutes the right to support by the system and ultimately by their tax-paying fellowmen. The term "insurance," in this respect, means public assistance.

A simple example may illustrate the case. Let us assume that a married person who regularly paid his payroll taxes since the initiation of the System retired after twenty years of coverage, on January 1, 1957. Let us also assume that he contributed the maximum payable under the law. From 1937 through 1949, he contributed 1 percent on $3,000 annual income, $30 per year, or a total of $390 in 13 years. In 1950, he paid 1½ percent on $3,600 or $72. In 1955 and 1956, his taxes amounted to 2 percent on $4,200 or a total of $168. Altogether he paid no more than $837 during the first 20 years of coverage. If we add an equal amount of "employer contribution," which actually came out of his pay, his total contribution to the System amounted to $1,674.

In 1957, this payment entitled a retiring couple to receive $162.80 in monthly benefits, which since then have been raised to $516 per month. In other words, in 1957 they received in ten months and eight days the equivalent of their total contributions. His life expectancy, however, amounted to approximately 13 years, hers to 18 years. If they were still alive in 1980, twenty-three years later, they were collecting every three months and eight days what they paid in since the beginning! Their total benefits have exceeded $50,000 on total contributions of $1,674 or 30 times more than they paid in.

Take a more recent example calculated by *U.S. News and World Report*. Assume that a married person retired on January 1, 1980. His wife also is 65. If he paid the maximum tax since the program started in 1937, Social Security took $11,202.97 in payroll taxes. His employer also paid that sum. He received no interest on his contribution, but he acquired an entitlement. In the first year of retirement, he received in benefits $11,154.90, almost as much as he paid in during the past forty-three years; and the benefits will keep coming, in larger and larger checks, as long as he lives. He, too, will receive more than he and his employer paid in.

How is it economically feasible that the Social Security Administration can pay many times more in benefits than it actually receives in contributions? Part of the answer is that, for many years, it merely extended the compulsory coverage to an ever widening circle of taxpayers. As long as additional millions of workers were added to the rolls, workers who were taxed, but remained ineligible for payments because they had not yet reached retirement age, the means for the beneficiaries' support were secured. At the same time, the System created more and more future liabilities to stay solvent for the moment. Moreover, both the tax rates and the taxable income of the working population were raised sharply in recent years. From January 1, 1937, to January 1, 1980, the maximum amount anyone could have contributed amounted to $11,202.97. In just six years, from January 1, 1980, to December 31, 1985, the lifetime total rocketed to $25,968; the annual exaction is scheduled to rise to $7,299.72 in 1989, which is the price the present generation of Americans must pay for the self-indulgence of its seniors. From $60 a year to $7,299.72 in just one generation—this is the progression of political entitlement and transfer once it has been unleashed. Moreover, according to the Social Security Administration itself, the actuarial deficit, or unfunded liability, amounts to more than $2.1 trillion, which forebodes much higher payroll taxes in the future.

The defenders of the System are quick to point at certain similarities between Social Security and private annuity. In both cases, they contend, beneficiaries who live longer than the calculated life expectancy on which the benefits are based actually receive more than they paid in; and beneficiaries who happen to pass away before they reach their expected age draw less or nothing at all. Unfortunately, this comparison between Social Security and private insurance is rather defective and deceptive. The numerous raises granted to Social Security beneficiaries did not come from its deceased members; life expectancy since 1937 has risen by several years, which, if adjustments are in order, would call for reductions of monthly benefits compensating for more benefit months. Private insurance, which lacks the power to tax and forcibly draw in more customers, cannot grant raises every year. In 1987, as in any other year, it would make the annuity payments it contracted to make in 1937; to double, triple and quadruple the benefits would invite loss and bankruptcy. Only a system that wields the power to tax and draft new members can become an agency of economic transfer and entitlement.

The Social Security System is promoting consumption and benefits for the present generation at the expense of future generations. On a massive scale, it redistributes income and wealth from young taxpayers to the older beneficiaries; it creates political classes of beneficiaries and victims.

Physicians, dentists, attorneys, corporate executives and other professional people, together with independent businessmen almost without exception belong to the class of victims. They are victimized especially because of the "earnings limits" from age 65 to 70. In spite of their accumulated contributions, workers lose their rights to a portion of their monthly benefits if they continue to earn $680 in monthly fees. Only when they reach an age of 70 are they entitled to their full benefits. It should be obvious that any physician who, at age 65, is on his feet and in possession of his faculties is earning more than $680 per month or $8,160 per year. He is taxed, but does not qualify for benefits until he is 70, when his life expectancy is much too short to recover the amount paid in during a long professional career.

The Social Security program taxes the professional class to support lower-income retirees. Even among the latter, it injures the active and diligent who prefer to continue working after 65. The laborer, too, loses his right to full monthly benefits if he should earn more than $680. He loses $1.00 in benefits for each additional $2.00 earned over $8,160 per year. In other words, to many workers after 65, it is more profitable to work only part time, merely earning supplementary income. Many others, especially the unskilled and untrained, do not work at all because the potential labor income is too small, when compared with Social Security benefits. They are reluctant to work because any labor exertion immediately reduces their benefits. In both cases, the System supports and encourages the inactivity of less productive workers with funds that are taken from more active people. These continue to be taxed, regardless of age, as long as they are rendering services and earning labor income.[4]

Born from the exploitation doctrine, the Social Security System is an open affront to the precepts of economics and morality. While it continues to be very popular with the benefit generation, it is resented by youth that is supposed to pay the benefits and cover the debt.

Assistance to Students

When compared with the entitlements of elderly Americans, which exceed $300 billion per year, the federal assistance to students is rather negligible; six current student aid programs provide just $15 billion in grants, subsidized work, and direct and guaranteed loans. Some 7 million post-secondary awards and loans are available to college, graduate and professional students or their parents, through federal student assistance programs. Loan guarantees provide over $9.3 billion in loans to some 3.8 million students or their parents. The loans are made at a subsidized rate, and students do not have to pay any interest while in school. Cash awards (Pell Grants) ranging from $200 to $1,600 are given to 1.8 million students. Under the summer youth employment program, grants are made to states, subsidizing minimum-wage government jobs and related training during the summer for youth between the ages of 14 and 21. The budget provided $725 million for the summer of 1986. Some 700,000 Vietnam Era veterans receive readjustment student benefits, at an annual cost of $1.3 billion. Some 10,000 wives and widows of Vietnam Era veterans and some 80,000 sons and daughters enjoy education assistance exceeding $300 million. About 720,000 students receive college work-study grants totalling more than $250 million, and traditionally, black colleges get direct grants in excess of $200 million every year.[5]

In the past twenty years, the cost of federal programs for students has exploded; more than half of all students now receive federally generated aid, which provides almost 20 percent of the cost of higher education in the United States and 50 percent of the educational cost of those students receiving aid. Moreover, state and local governments, in 1986, spent an estimated $190 billion on education, of which some $35 billion was allocated to higher education.[6] In 1956, fewer than 3 million students attended colleges and universities; in 1966, the number had doubled. By 1986, it had doubled again, soaring to an estimated 12,162,000 of whom 9,533,000 were enrolled in government institutions.[7]

The American people, and their policy makers in Washington, apparently are committed to the idea of a universal college education for all. To undertake such a commitment, government must allocate the resources necessary to impart the education. It must contrive new impositions and exact more revenue from the population that is already laboring under heavy tax burdens. Once again, it must call upon judges, tax collectors and sheriffs to collect income and wealth from some people so that others may benefit. In the final analysis, government resorts to brute force, which casts serious doubt on the morality of its educational programs.

It is a basic principle of political economy that government can augment and magnify that which it subsidizes. Through grants, loans and other incentives, it may draw individuals, young and old, to college campuses. In fact, it may send everyone to college, just as 50 years ago it managed to give everyone a high school education, and 50 years earlier an eighth grade education. To make a college education available to all is to adjust the standard of quality to all, which is the lowest common denominator. The college degree merely takes the place of the high school diploma, which took the place of the eighth grade diploma. In the end, while government, on all its levels, spends massive sums of taxpayer money, the college degree becomes a meaningless rank earned through faithful attendance at a custodial institution of government or licensed by government.

Before the age of government education, characterized by truancy laws and school levies, the aim of education was to know the laws of God in nature and revelation, and then to fashion human affection and action into harmony with those laws. Education did not merely consist of mastering a science or foreign language, but was found in the study of the general nature of morals and of the specific moral choices to be made by the individual in his relationship with others. The principles of right or good conduct as revealed in Scripture were the standards of a genuinely liberal education. Government education, unfortunately, denies and rejects such standards. It lives by its own standards, which are political, enacted by politicians and enforced by judges and policemen. It has given us the largest government school system on earth, the most expensive college buildings, and the most extensive curriculum, but has cast out the source of all knowledge—God Himself. Instead, it worships politics and idolizes the men who direct the affairs of the world.

Government institutions of learning openly profess an interest in education for moral and spiritual values, by which they mean those values that bring individual behavior into accord with "the standards of conduct that are approved in our democratic culture." In other words, democratic culture gives rise to standards of conduct; democracy, which is the practice of self-government, provides the cultural framework for the development of standards. In short, public opinion and majority vote are the source of values. The voice of the majority is the voice of God.[8]

Help for the Needy

The voice of the people, we are told, calls for redistribution of income and wealth on a massive scale. It calls upon the federal government to tax and restrain productive people, and promote others who are deemed to be truly in need. Government is to be a transfer agency, transferring income from the relatively well-to-do to the relatively poor.

To find the poor and needy, the U.S. government applies a crude yardstick. The Department of Agriculture determines the cost of nutritionally adequate food for a family and then multiplies the amount by 3, on the assumption that food expenses comprise approximately one-third of a poor family's expenditures. Every year, adjustments are made in the poverty income level on the basis of changes in the Consumer Price Index.

The government yardstick of poverty is as arbitrary and unsatisfactory as all other yardsticks that are to measure individual needs or comforts, the lack of which is said to indicate poverty. Most poor Americans are enjoying material amenities for which most human beings envy them; they do not know that they are poor unless they are told by poverty officials. Millions of farmers throughout American history did not earn an amount three times the cost of the food they consumed; and yet, they deemed them-selves blessed and well-to-do. Millions of individuals who practice mutual assistance and barter may not earn the threshhold income, and yet, may enjoy material amenities far in excess of the poverty line. Millions of individuals who live on their savings may feel so affluent that they no longer generate income, which would place them right in the poverty class. Many families choosing to spend half of their meager incomes on education for their children may have little left for food; they may not live by the nutritional standards of the U.S. Department of Agriculture, and yet, rejoice in their great blessings, deeming themselves wealthy in the number of things by which they are loved and blessed. On the other hand, individuals earning more than three times the threshhold income may feel deprived and impoverished because their thirst of desire is never filled. They may even feel the pains of poverty because country club dues are boosted and living expenses other than food are rising. Where restrictive housing legislation causes rents to soar, and efficiency apartments rent at $1,000 or more per week, an income of four or five times the food budget may not cover the rent. People may freeze in cars, campgrounds, shacks, and tents, and yet exceed the threshhold income.

The measure of poverty, nevertheless, may serve a useful func-tion by signaling increases or decreases in poverty as per capita incomes rise or fall. When real income rises, as it has done throughout most of U.S. history, more and more individuals earn incomes in excess of a given poverty line. When real income declines, as it has throughout most of the 1970s and 1980s, more and more individuals are bound to fall below the line and appear in the class of the officially poor. The poverty measure thus may reveal not only the trend of real income, but also the effectiveness of government policies that mean to promote economic develop-ment and alleviate poverty. In particular, it may be useful in judging "the war on poverty," which President Johnson declared in 1964 and every U.S. President has waged ever since.

Before the war on poverty, approximately thirteen percent of the population were officially poor. After hundreds of billions of dollars had been spent on social welfare programs, more than fifteen percent now are poor. Before the war on poverty, more than seven million Americans were dependent on public assistance; twenty years later, some six million Americans were living on permanent welfare and another twelve million on temporary welfare programs. The war on poverty obviously aggravated the lot of the poor. According to some observers, it turned into a war on the poor by victimizing its supposed beneficiaries in a number of ways.

Most government welfare programs are designed to create beneficiaries and render them dependent and helpless. They make poverty an institution that is perpetuated by legions of politicians and government officials. Public programs create a new class of poverty administrators who consume the lion's share of the poverty budget. It is estimated that only thirty cents of the anti-poverty dollar actually go to the poor; seventy cents are spent on overhead and administration.[9]

Government welfare programs contribute to the disintegration of poor families. They make women and children dependent on government; dependent for food, for clothing, for shelter; and reward fatherless families with extra benefits and welfare perks. With welfare families in disarray, the only dependable escape route from poverty—family effort and support—is obstructed and blocked.

Government welfare programs actually create incentives for idleness. Every increase in transfer income reduces the disutility of idleness and creates a shift from payrolls to welfare rolls. When welfare benefits finally exceed the wages which poorly trained and poorly educated workers can earn, it is only sensible that many choose to be unemployed and dependent. In many centers of poverty, the sum of public assistance, housing subsidy, foodstamps, and Medicaid significantly exceeds the wage that can be earned through labor exertion.

Labor laws and regulations, finally, may bar poor people from competing in the labor market. They erect formidable barriers such as the minimum wage, occupational licenses, union power and privilege, and the regulation of the taxi and trucking trades. Labor legislation prevents social mobility because it does not permit poor people to get on the bottom rung of the economic ladder.[10]

Government is rather ill-suited and poorly equipped to alleviate the plight of the poor. It lacks moral rules or standards, and is devoid of basic principles in economic and social matters. Its guiding lights are public opinion and majority vote; its modus operandi is law and law enforcement. Its primary function, as judged by its revenues and expenditures, is that of a transfer agency engaged in distributing benefits and allocating burdens. It transfers income and wealth according to the rules of politics, which make politicians the primary beneficiaries of the system, and the poor and needy the primary victims.

Subsidies for Farmers

American farmers are both victims and beneficiaries. The farm crisis is as old as the transfer system itself. At the present, it is costing American taxpayers more than $28 billion per year, and American consumers even more, through planting restrictions and output limitations, through giveaways and subsidized sales to foreigners, or just through storage that causes the supplies to rot in government silos and warehouses.[11] After all, what is an agricultural surplus? A quantity of food withdrawn from the market and withheld from consumers. Surely, such tactics mean to benefit American farmers. Unfortunately, they bring about the very opposite of what they set out to achieve. They have brought, and continue to bring, much poverty and despair to rural America.

The objective of many government programs may be laudable, indeed. "Federal programs," so the 1987 Budget reads, "help meet domestic and international trade demand for food and fiber while mitigating the adverse effects of price fluctuations on farmers."[12] The net result, unfortunately, is the very opposite. The U.S. programs tend to withdraw food and fiber from the domestic and international markets, and reduce the supplies by restricting production through quotas and other devices. The programs also aggravate the price fluctuations by creating surpluses and having them managed by politicians and bureaucrats. The overall net result is ever higher federal expenditures and taxpayer outlays, while agricultural sales at home and abroad decline.

Some ninety-two percent of estimated 1987 federal agricultural expenditures are "to stabilize farm income." There are the commodity price support programs created to stabilize, support, and protect farm income and prices. The Department of Agriculture, working through the Commodity Credit Corporation, sets target prices, provides income support and deficiency payments, and offers special loans to farmers. There is the Federal Crop Insurance Corporation that offers insurance to producers against crop losses from natural hazards such as excessive rainfall or drought. There is the Farmers Home Administration that provides some fifteen percent of total farm credit. There are the agricultural research efforts and services, such as the extension program, the marketing program, and the plant health program. They all redirect farmers' attention and efforts toward politics, legislation and regulation, and cause farmers to lose sight of the only dependable source of prosperity: consumers. To deviate from the wishes and orders of consumers, and to follow the commands and enticements of politicians and their agents, is to invite great pain and suffering in the end.

The ethical rules or standards governing the conduct of agricultural policies are borrowed from the realm of politics. They are the rules of might over right, majority will over minority protection, and the power to create "economic rights" for some people by making demands and imposing obligations on other people.

Foreign Aid

From 1945 until today, the U.S. government may have given more than half a trillion dollars to foreign governments to achieve "a world order that provides peace, security, and prosperity." In fiscal year 1987 alone, it requested a budget authority of $22.6 billion in new foreign aid funds. It estimated its foreign credits to exceed $68 billion, and its guaranteed loans to top $20 billion.[13]

No matter what we may think of the effectiveness of this massive U.S. foreign aid, the world today undoubtedly is less peaceful and less secure than at any time since World War II. "Wars of liberation" are raging continually, while the superpowers are standing always ready to annihilate each other and much of the world. Yet, American political leaders cling to their aid programs, spouting old and stale justifications for their policies, in particular, waxing eloquent about military, political, and humanitarian ends.

The latter were best expressed by President Kennedy in his 1963 foreign aid message to Congress: "The richest nation in the world would surely be justified in spending less than one percent of its national income on assistance to its less fortunate sister nations solely as a matter of international responsibility."

One can be motivated by military, political, and humanitarian considerations, and yet deny the advisability of foreign aid. Its effects may be objectionable for both the donor and the recipient. Whether it is federal aid to domestic industries or economic aid to foreigners, it puts politicians in the driver's seat, and employs an army of bureaucrats to manage the truck. It may lead people to rely on politicians for economic improvement and development, and may reconfirm their faith in politics as the ultimate source of economic well-being.

Foreign aid is intergovernmental aid that strengthens the hand of politicians, especially in the recipient countries, breeds bureaucracies, and fosters government enterprises. In the underdeveloped areas of the world, where the private-property order has never been tried, it may even be fatal; for it obscures the only durable road toward economic improvement, which is individual initiative and the profit system. This is the urgent message by P. T. (Lord) Bauer, whose brilliant analysis, titled the *Third World and Economic Delusion*, demonstrates a high correlation between the amount of U.S. aid received and the economic follies committed by politicians and bureaucrats.[14] It points at a myriad of objectives, such as military production or procurement, expropriation of land and facilities of production, construction of government enterprises, subsidies to government-owned or government-regulated industries such as railroads and airlines, electric, gas, and power facilities, public housing, etc. etc. The objective is economic reorganization along the lines of a political command system; foreign aid is helping to bring it about.

Surely, the economic needs are rather dire and urgent. A railroad system that is owned by government and managed by officials undoubtedly is in urgent need of repair. Public utilities that are government-owned or government-run, suffering blackouts and brownouts, are in need of reconstruction. A government-owned telephone system that has more difficulties making across-the-street connections than a private company has making intercontinental connections undoubtedly is in a sad state. Where government practices strict rent control, housing conditions undoubtedly are deplorable and in need of repair. Yet, the desperate need for economic reconstruction does not call for the apparatus of politics to take charge of the economic lives of the people. On the contrary, it calls for maximum individual freedom and economic effort. Lasting improvement cannot come from foreign aid, which is similar to domestic aid. Genuine improvement necessitates eliminating the root of the evil: political control over economic activity.

U.S. foreign aid is openly promoting socialism, and unwittingly paving the way for world communism. The Alliance for Progress, which President Kennedy spearheaded with nineteen Latin American countries, expressly calls for long-term central planning. The member governments are to stimulate economic growth through deficit spending and credit expansion. The Alliance charter envisions international commodity agreements involving the cooperation of all member governments to enforce rigid price controls on producers and consumers alike. The tax levies on more productive members of society are to be raised to achieve a political distribution of income and wealth. Private land holdings are to be expropriated to achieve land tenure and food production according to political plan.

The U.S. government grants massive aid to governments that expropriate American-owned companies, seize American bank accounts, expel American citizens, and cancel debts to American citizens or government. It supports ruthless dictators who nationalize the means of production and slaughter their political opponents. It granted aid to Pol Pot, the butcher of two million Cambodians, to Idi Amin when he was slaughtering Ugandans, to Mugave when his troups annihilated his country's minorities, to Mengister of Ethiopia, who is deliberately starving millions of Ethiopians to death. The United States even financed the Communist dictatorship of Afghanistan, which called upon the USSR to invade and occupy the country. In short, the record of U.S. foreign aid is not just dismal, it is perverse. More than any other federal policy, it seems to reveal a deep death wish by many liberal politicians and government officials who apparently are blinded by pernicious creeds and doctrines, lost in confusion and futility, and bewildered in their intellectual identity. Cut loose from the moorings of the private property order, which is the mainspring of Western civilization, they flounder in the dark. The dim light they see points toward the command system; foreign aid is a broad path toward that light.

Aid to Others

A myriad of other paths leads in the same direction. The federal government regulates the capital markets; it promotes some uses of capital and restricts others. It provides funds to rearrange the mortgage market through the Government National Mortgage Association (GNMA), the Federal Housing Administration (FHA), Housing for the Elderly or Handicapped (Section 202), the Farmers Home Administration (FmHA), the Federal Deposit Insurance Corporation, the Federal Savings and Loan Insurance Corp., the National Credit Union Administration, the Small Business Administration (SBA), the Minority Business Development Agency (MBDA). The federal government seeks to promote and maintain transportation services and facilities through highway construction, highway safety, mass transit, and railroad programs. It is responsible for the improvement, operation, and maintenance of the national airspace system, makes airport grants, and finances aeronautical research and the operation of two airports (National and Dulles) in the Washington, D.C., area. It subsidizes water transportation through search and rescue services, maintenance of navigation aids, grants to the merchant marine and shipbuilding industries so that they may compete with foreign maritime industries, and makes direct loans and guaranteed loans for water and ground transportation. "To maintain the economic vitality and general well-being of society," the federal government finances programs for community and regional development. The Department of Housing and Urban Development's (HUD) block grant program provides federal support for cities, counties, Indian tribes, and U.S. territories. The Department makes urban development action grants, rental rehabilitation grants, rental development grants, and conducts assistance programs through the Economic Development Administration (EDA), the Bureau of Indian Affairs, the Appalachian Regional Commission (ARC), and the Tennessee Valley Authority (TVA). The federal government allocates funds to ensure strength in science and space technology. It conducts programs through the National Science Foundation, the National Aeronautics and Space Administration, and the Department of Energy. "To supply energy at reasonable prices," the federal government conducts research and development programs, directs production programs, and subsidizes synthetic fuels, electric utilities, and telephone systems. It is building a strategic petroleum reserve (SPR) and supporting the work of the Nuclear Regulatory Commission. It conducts energy grant programs for the purpose of weatherizing school buildings, hospitals, and the homes of low income families. Finally, "to achieve a world order that provides peace, security, and prosperity," the federal government provides international security assistance, development, humanitarian and refugee assistance through the Agency for International Development, the Export-Import Bank, foreign military sales trust fund, the Economic Support Fund, and international organizations.[15]

Unfortunately, it is not in the power of government to make everyone more prosperous. Government can only raise the income of one person by taking from another; however, the taking and giving are not a zero net game. They require an elaborate apparatus of transfer that may consume a large share of the taking. Both the giving and the taking may adversely affect the productive efforts of both the beneficiaries and the victims; but even if they were robots and should remain unaffected by the process, the cost of the transfer apparatus alone would substantially reduce total economic well-being. Moreover, the transfer process does not ensue from a coordinated policy of income transfer. Each department and agency of government pursues its own policy against the endeavors of the other departments and agencies. The Department of Labor seeks to raise wage rates and to lower living costs. The Department of Agriculture fights to raise food prices; similarly the Department of Commerce endeavors to reduce foreign imports and raise domestic goods prices. The Department of Housing and Urban Development seeks to provide low-cost housing; both the Department of Labor and the Department of the Treasury significantly boost housing costs. The former imposes costly labor regulations, the latter indulges in deficit spending that deprives the mortgage market of needed funds and raises interest rates. One agency of government fights against monopoly, but many other agencies create public monopolies of their own and bring about conditions that invite monopolistic restraint.

The various departments and agencies of government act as spokesmen and public defenders of special interest groups engaged in a perpetual political struggle. In its own way, each office seeks to promote its own interests at the expense of others. They all wax eloquent about urgent needs and great emergencies while they are preying on each other. If there were truth in politics, they would be forced to reveal that every new promise they make to their special constituents constitutes a new threat of exaction and pain to all others.

3

THE ETHICS OF ENTITLEMENT

Equitable Distribution

It was not always the function of government to take income and wealth from its wealthy citizenry and confer entitlements on others. The U.S. government assumed the task only two generations ago, when Congress introduced progressive taxation and, soon thereafter, launched systems of old age insurance and unemployment compensation. Since then, social pressure, sustained by strong moral emotion, has caused all administrations to pursue the ideal of an equal distribution of the goods of this world.

From its very beginning, some economists have strenuously opposed all political efforts at redistribution. They point not only at the tremendous rise in economic well-being of all social classes, including the poor and disabled, long before governments embarked upon income redistribution, but also at the futility of all such policies. The working and living conditions of American workers, they contend, were the best in the world long before New Deal legislators passed labor laws. In the United States, they remind us, even individuals existing on public assistance have always lived better by far than their peers in other countries. American economic history clearly attests to the tremendous productivity which a system of economic freedom unleashes. Mindful of the phenomenal improvement in the living conditions of every citizen of a free society, of the reduction in human mortality rates and the great lengthening of life expectancy, the foes of redistribution proudly conclude that unhampered economic freedom is most virtuous and moral. The system of social organization that builds on freedom is in complete harmony with the calls and imperatives of ethics.

These economists are unalterably opposed to political intervention because it springs from politics, builds on verdicts and interpretations of judges, and depends on brute enforcement by police. It runs counter to the inexorable laws of human action and, therefore, brings forth the very opposite of what it sets out to achieve. It hampers economic production, discourages individual effort, stifles economic progress, and creates social and economic classes whose self-interests are irreconcilable. Government intervention on behalf of one social class against another not only is illogical and ineffective, but also highly immoral. It defies the Eighth Commandment—Thou shalt not steal—and violates the Tenth Commandment—Thou shalt not covet anything that is thy neighbor's. It is bound to bring poverty, frustration, quarrel, and strife.

The advocates of redistribution remain undaunted by such rejoinders. They reinterpret and reject the evidence, and cling to doctrines and theories of their own. They raise the question of the goodness and desirability of redistribution for the benefit of the greatest number. Searching for fairness and brotherly love, they pursue two distinct ideals: the removal of human want and suffering through the use of economic surplus, and the abolition of the great inequality of means among the several members of society.

Removal of Want

Many redistributionists like to give vivid descriptions of the sad conditions of impoverished and destitute members of society. They point at the chronically unemployed and underemployed lacking money or means for an adequate existence. They wax eloquent about their fellow men who are abjectly and conspicuously poor, and who, suffering hunger and want due to misfortune, are in urgent need of assistance. After all, man has a moral obligation to help his unfortunate fellow men. This duty rests squarely on the Judeo-Christian ideal of brotherhood that makes every man his brother's keeper. To act in accordance with the standards and precepts of Judeo-Christian codes of behavior is to be a Good Samaritan.

A helper and benefactor to the unfortunate and poor, the Good

Samaritan binds the wounds, nurses the sick and helps them get back on their feet. He *does not* call for government programs that make poverty a permanent social institution, playing a central role in politics. He *does not* favor progressive income taxation, nor depend on poverty administrators consuming the lion's share of the poverty budget, or poverty politicians enacting minimum wage laws, occupational licensing, and union power and privilege. To be a helper indeed is to lend a friendly hand to a needy person; it is personal effort and sacrifice.

To pool their efforts and maximize their effectiveness, Good Samaritans may want to cooperate with each other in church congregations and other charitable organizations. Yet, they must be ever mindful that any delegation of charitable obligations may reduce the quality of charity and, in the end, deny it altogether. To rush by a poor man who fell among thieves and later send a few dollars to a world relief organization is to pass by on the other side, like the priest and the Levite. The Good Samaritan does not ride on, but places the victim on his own beast, brings him to an inn, and takes care of him.

The advocates of redistribution ride on, pointing at the pitiful conditions of the laboring classes during the eighteenth and nineteenth centuries, and hailing labor legislators and labor organizers for having brought about remarkable improvements. They pin their faith to politics and labor unions. Unfortunately, both are utterly incapable of improving the economic conditions of all laborers. If they could, the poverty of Africa, Asia, and Latin America would be outlawed tomorrow. Labor unions in Bolivia and Columbia, instead of seeking benefits just for members, at the expense of nonmembers, could demand more for all workers and get more. The governments of Gabon, Sri Lanka, and Tanzania could adopt and enforce minimum wage laws just like those in the United States, could introduce Social Security and Medicare just like those in the United States, and thereby bring American prosperity to their wretched masses. Actually, neither these foreign governments nor the U.S. government can improve the lot of working people. Economic conditions spring from and depend on economic production. To improve labor and living conditions is to increase labor productivity. It requires a will and courage to work, save, and invest, and a respect for private property in the means of production.

The redistributionists ride on, calling for the distribution of surplus wealth and pointing at more affluent members of society. They are aware that the moral obligation to help the poor and needy rests most heavily, although not exclusively, on the wealthy, but they are grossly misinformed about the magnitude and value of the surplus wealth that is available for redistribution. In a commercial and industrial society, nearly all personal wealth consists of means of production, affording jobs and providing consumer goods for the people. The great wealth of an American billionaire consists of oil wells and refineries, means of transportation and communication, founder's stock and growth stock, debenture bonds and mortgage bonds. To seize his productive assets and consume them is to reduce labor productivity, lower wage rates, and aggravate the plight of the poor. It is rather counterproductive, no matter whether it is exacted by progressive income taxation or confiscatory estate levies.

Equalization of Incomes

Many redistributionists nevertheless favor progressive taxation because they are more concerned about the inequalities of income and wealth than the alleviation of poverty. They are troubled by the sorry conditions of the unemployed classes, but they are even more apprehensive about the unequal distribution of wealth. It is highly improper and unjust, they argue, that some people have less than is necessary, while others have so much more. Some individuals suffer hunger and want, while others dwell in idle luxury; the poor live in alleys and cellar ways, while the rich frequent nightclubs, casinos and horse races. In fact, it is scandalous that so many should live in dire need while others indulge in "silly" expenditures. This is why many redistributionists favor a floor beneath which no one should be left and a ceiling above which no one should be permitted to rise.

It is a popular habit of speech to call "just" that which people desire and "unjust" that which they disapprove. They clamor for economic equality in the name of justice, although justice actually demands inequality. Justice means due reward or treatment. It grants individual rewards proportionate to individual effort and assigns to every individual the fruits of his labor. It is therefore reasonable to conclude that justice is not served by compulsory equalization of incomes, and that, contrary to public opinion, our present society, engaged in redistribution by political force, is not a just society.

The forces of equalization do not spring from justice, but from two absolute disapprovals by public opinion makers: the unrightness of hunger and want, and the unrightness of luxury. Redistribution is supposed to bring forth a righteous society. Sacrificing nothing of value, it is to overcome the evil of want by suppressing the evil of luxury. It is to correct one bad pattern of life—poverty—by the suppression of another bad pattern—luxury.

Egalitarians are ill-informed about the quantity of idle wealth that can be seized and distributed. As mentioned above, great personal wealth consists primarily of productive capital, the expropriation and consumption of which reduces labor productivity and labor income. Surpluses consisting of idle luxuries in the hands of the rich are inadequate by far to raise lower incomes to a desirable level. The pursuit of equality, when conducted in earnest, therefore, involves the lowering of all incomes, even those of skilled workers and lower-middle-class producers. In the end, policies of income equalization merely rearrange income horizontally; they do not, as is commonly believed, redistribute much income and wealth from the rich to the poor.

Redistributionists like to base their case on "the economics of welfare," which teaches that a loss of the last unit of income of the affluent is but a small sacrifice; but the same unit in the hands of the poor amounts to a substantial improvement. Professor Pigou states it most succinctly: "It is evident that any transference of income from a relatively rich man to a relatively poor man of similar temperament, since it enables more intense wants to be satisfied at the expense of less intense wants, must increase the aggregate sum of satisfactions."[1] Professor Lerner repeats the principle in an academic garb: "Total satisfaction is maximized by that division of incomes which equalizes the marginal utilities of income of all the individuals in the society."[2] In the end, he and his welfare colleagues arrive at the conclusion that "the probable value of total satisfactions is maximized by dividing income evenly."[3]

It is difficult to fathom the inner-direction that leads these professors to such popular, though erroneous, conclusions. It can readily be seen that the utilities of income of different persons cannot be measured with a common rod. No one can measure the utility of the last dollar of income of one person and then compare it with its utility in the hands of another person. We do know, however, that the intensity of the dissatisfaction due to loss of income and sudden lowering of levels of living may be far greater than the satisfaction from receiving largesse. The victim of the transfer process may be more indignant about the loss than the beneficiary is cheerful and contented about his gain. Psychologists warn of the violent, socially disruptive discontent of individuals who are suddenly deprived of their customary ways of life. In fact, being victimized by unjust policies that depress some people at the expense of others may create the emotional ingredients from which revolutions are made. The wrath of the victims may be the spark that ignites the powder keg which is the transfer system.

In democratic societies with a long tradition of majority rule, the dissatisfaction of the victims does not readily ignite the political powder keg, as long as the transfer beneficiaries outnumber the victims. The minority is accustomed to living by the decisions of the majority, not because they are believed to be fair and just, but because submission safeguards the peace. To rise and rebel against it would mean conflict and violence, to which the friends of democracy are unwilling to resort. Yet, throughout the nondemocratic world, accustomed to political conflict and rule by brute force, attempts at income redistribution often lead to violence. The political minority that is to be sacrificed to majority entitlements searches for ways to escape or, when all avenues of escape are barred, to strike back at the majority; acting through juntas of colonels and generals, for example, it may seize political power and establish its own transfer system.

In democratic societies, the dissatisfaction caused by loss of income can be observed in the political opposition to measures of redistribution. Successful opposition denotes an excess of dissatisfaction; token opposition signals continuing support for redistribution. Successful resistance may reveal that most voters now see themselves as victims, rather than beneficiaries; token opposition may signal voter belief that redistribution continues to benefit them. It should be borne in mind, however, that the relative strength of both the transfer and the antitransfer party is affected not only by their personal gains or losses, but also by considerations of moral imperatives. Even the victim of redistribution may at times cast his vote for an entitlement if he deems it moral and righteous; similarly, the beneficiary may vote against it and refuse to accept it if he believes it to be wrong.

Unheeded Consequences

Most of the time, the beneficiaries can be expected to press for redistribution in carefree disregard of its effects on society. They blithely assume that economic activity will continue undiminished, no matter what government may do to the producer, that productive capital will be created, jobs provided and wage rates be raised, regardless of the exactions from savers and investors. Obviously, such assumptions spring from wishful thinking and economic daydreaming. Redistribution that seriously aims at equality tends to retard economic progress, bring about stagnation and recession, and, in the end, lead to universal scarcity through capital consumption.

Redistributionists who refuse to see such basic effects also are oblivious to more subtle effects that tend to render redistribution rather counterproductive. Three such effects deserve immediate attention. First, confiscatory tax levies may cause individuals with exceptional energy and ability, the entrepreneurs and captains of industry, to leave economic life and pursue other vocations. In an unhampered market order, many highly talented individuals are led to serve the economic needs and wants of the people. In the service of consumers, who are the sovereign bosses of the market order, they are free to apply their energy and ability to revolutionize and reorganize every phase of production. Following their own interests and motives, they may interact with competitors, acting as buyers and sellers, users and producers of goods and services. In freedom, inventors like Eli Whitney and

Thomas Edison, innovators like Andrew Carnegie and Henry Ford, and organizers like Edward Harriman and Pierpont Morgan are led to mobilize economic resources and direct them toward serving the public. The vital few, instead of ruling men, are led to serve men.[4]

Individual freedom reveals inequality in productivity, which brings forth inequality in income. Confiscatory tax levies, designed to redistribute income and wealth, not only repress individual freedom, but also run counter to human nature. They are supposed to achieve what is not in human nature. Moreover, they prevent many gifted people from pursuing their careers in economic life, and cause them to seek self-fulfillment in the arts and sciences, in civil service or military careers, or in the pursuit of national, racial and political objectives. These levies may force creative people to surrender economic management to politicians and bureaucrats. The detrimental effects on economic well-being need not be elaborated.

Second, redistribution deprives society of the great variety of life styles and cultural and intellectual activities that spring from various life styles. It brings about a radical shift in demand and production. The demand for and production of popular goods and services is bound to rise; production for the affluent classes is destined to shrink. In particular, the production of artistic and intellectual goods is likely to be affected; operas, symphonies, chamber music, painting, sculpturing, and other manifestations of the fine arts face dwindling markets. In fact, man's cultural aspirations may suffer serious losses unless government provides a new superstructure of cultural activities, maintaining and promoting common interest through public libraries, theaters and opera houses, and public centers of fine arts. Government must grant scholarships and fellowships to artists and scientists, and otherwise provide generous support for creative activities normally sustained and promoted by people in higher income brackets. Government must make investments in individual talents that render services in medicine, engineering, and education. At great expense, it must create and maintain a new elite that will serve the masses. It must repair the social damage inflicted by the reduction of upper-and middle-class incomes.

Government repair efforts, however, not only necessitate higher public expenditures and taxation, but also run counter to the very purpose of redistribution, the maximization of individual satisfactions through income equalization. In search of the "good society," all such efforts promote the production of goods and services for which there is meager demand and, thereby, bring about the very allocation of resources that generated the clamor for redistribution. If income equalization maximizes the sum of want satisfactions, all state expenditures in support of cultural and professional activity blatantly disregard the maximization principle and openly contradict the very rationale of redistribution.

Third, the redistribution process, as well as the repair effort that may follow, places politicians and government officials in the center of the economic order. To seize income and wealth from individuals with higher incomes, politicians must pass laws, judges must adjudicate them, and policemen enforce them. Having amputated the higher incomes, which provide the savings and investments for economic growth, politicians and officials must assume the saving and investment functions. When desirable social activities are declining, they must provide for and preside over these activities. When personal income becomes insufficient for expensive training and education, they must select the trainees and provide the necessary funds. In every case, redistribution leads to an expansion of the powers of government and of the individuals who run the government—politicians and officials. Redistribution requires an apparatus of redistribution, which is government; the consequences of redistribution in turn necessitate a repair effort that calls for more government, making politicians and government officials the primary beneficiaries of redistribution.

Pure redistribution would require a simple negative income tax that hands lower-income people that which is taken from higher-income people, but this is not the redistribution that is practiced. Politicians and officials act as trustees of the "under-privileged," assigning the burdens and doling out the benefits. To avoid creation of a class of unproductive wards, whose civil rights would soon be curtailed, the entitlement benefits are extended to all members of society. Social Security and Medicare benefits are extended to the rich and the poor alike, which significantly raises the expenses of redistribution. The extension of benefits to all, in turn, warrants an extension of tax exactions from all. In the end, low income earners, along with individuals in high-income brackets, tend to contribute more to the system than they receive from it; after all, the legions of administrators need to be supported promptly and fittingly.

The great beneficiary of the redistribution ideology is government. It helps government to break down the age-old resistance of taxpayers to a larger government share of economic production and income. For centuries, the people had resisted successfully and, in many cases, had risen in revolution against governments seeking to increase their shares; but this resistance that gave power to parliament and brought forth political liberty crumbled under the onslaught of the redistribution ideology. It shattered the solidarity of taxpayers through increasing inequality of treatment, deductions, allowances, credits, and positive benefits for individuals in lower-income brackets. Unfortunately, it also divided society into two social classes: the beneficiaries of transfer, who are calling for ever more; and the victims, who submit unwillingly. It could hardly fail to injure social peace and harmony.

Envy or Error

The conflict society does not spring from the desire to improve the economic and social standards of its poorer members. It is the bitter fruit of egalitarian ideals that call for equalization of incomes through the agency of the redistributing state. These ideals do not necessarily reject and condemn all economic inequality; they find fault only with the income and wealth of entrepreneurs and capitalists. Egalitarianism does not necessarily flow from envy and covetousness, but rests precariously on economic error that perceives capitalist income as exploitation profit filched from the people.

Throughout the ages, man, as member of the body politic, has readily accepted the pomp and splendor of his ruler. He may have opposed his king when the royal exactions became oppressive and his policies reckless and foolish. Subjects may have risen in open rebellion when the yoke became unbearable, but if we read history aright, the people were rarely, if ever, led to rise against their duly established government for reasons of envy or covetousness. The most diverse societies have tolerated economic inequality quite willingly.

Surely, many people are uneasy and envious of the attainments of others, but few Americans resent the magnificent spectacle of government grandeur displayed so ostentatiously in Washington, D.C. Every year, millions of people are drawn to the temples of politics that fill them with awe and admiration. They do not begrudge their leaders the luxuries of political office; they cheerfully approve of the imperial conditions of their President, their senators and representatives, no matter how mediocre they may be. Similarly, most Americans do not for a moment covet the million-dollar incomes of their favorite artists, entertainers, singers and athletes. They love and cherish their favorite film stars, crooners, and quarterbacks, and expect them to make a gallant spectacle of their success.

The same people who so readily accept the entertainer's accomplishment and the politician's position in the body politic may resent the capitalist's income for being "unearned" and "unjust." They may be resentful of the fortunes earned by the manufacturer of men's shoes or lady's stockings, of toothpaste or mouthwash. In their eyes, such fortunes are dirty lucre withheld from workers and gouged from consumers. They cling to popular notions that give rise to the doctrines of egalitarianism and to policies of redistribution.

The antagonistic attitudes toward exceptional income and personal wealth rest precariously on a misunderstanding of the market process; in particular, the determination of wage rates and entrepreneurial income. They may also draw on man's sense of justice that justifies exceptional incomes on grounds of individual excellence and superiority. Unfortunately, man's vision of excellence is rather limited; while he recognizes it in his favorite entertainers and football players, he does not perceive it in the producer of his favorite toothpaste and mouthwash. At any rate, he is rather reluctant to acknowledge any excellence in the satisfaction of such basic needs which fully occupy most people. Even if he should recognize excellence in common pursuits and occupations, he is likely to discount its importance. A young man may admire and love his baseball idol and simultaneously view the manufacturer of his idol's shoes and stockings with contempt. Similarly, he may admire his favorite politician, living in regal splendor and the glare of publicity, being dimly aware that the agents of government always have been unequal, authoritative, and superior. Although their splendor is generally derived from levies and exactions from the populace, while the exceptional incomes of entrepreneurs and capitalists stem from production and voluntary exchange, he readily accepts politicians and officials as his leaders and superiors, but refuses to grant similar recognition to entrepreneurs and capitalists.

Intellectual consistency is no great concern for redistributionists. In their own economic lives, they often choose and prefer essential want satisfaction over entertainment and politics, allocating more of their incomes to the production of shoes, stockings, toothpaste and mouthwash than to baseball and football, and casting their economic votes for the best producers. As members of the body politic, however, they would like to negate their own economic actions and redistribute the producers' income.

Ignorance deprives man of his freedom, for he does not know what alternatives there are. He is unlikely to choose that which he has never heard of. This is why economic education offers the only cure for certain diseases the modern world has engendered. It refutes and explodes all egalitarian ideas and the demand for equalization of incomes, for they do not lead to economic equality, but to ever more inequality, political power, and social strife.

4

UNDERGROUND GOVERNMENT

Going Off-Budget

When the burden of taxation becomes oppressive, many tax-payers are tempted to evade their obligations by working off-the-books. When government regulations and license requirements make certain services exorbitantly expensive, many people may disregard the restrictions and hire unlicensed labor, or learn to do it themselves. When entitlement benefits are connected with employment and income restrictions, the beneficiaries are tempted to ignore the restrictions and work off-the-books. In every case, people react to the burdens imposed and obstacles erected by hiding from the watchful eyes of political authorities and escaping to the underground.

In a similar way, when constraints on government pose a major threat to politicians, government employees and powerful interest groups that benefit from political largess, government goes underground. When budget cuts threaten the position and income of politicians and bureaucrats, they react by going "off budget." Whether they are committed philosophically to expanding the political arena, or just to defending their economic existence and life style, off-budget operations are an important procedure for achieving their goal.

The path to underground government is rather short and direct. Government merely needs to establish independent corporations, that is, quasi-public enterprises, that are managed by politicians or their appointees and operated "off-budget." These enterprises (OBEs) may engage in any economic activity from the construction and maintenance of airports, public housing and libraries, to the development of theaters, stadiums and zoos. Their spending, borrowing, and other activities are deleted from any government budget and official statistics. Their debt is not subject to a constitutional debt limitation, nor is it conditional on voter approval. Government activity may thus be made to disappear by a simple stroke of the pen that creates a corporate charter. The simple expedient of a corporate guise moves political machinations beyond the control and scrutiny of the electorate.[1]

An OBE is a creation of politics. It is a body or board authorized by law to enact ordinances or adopt resolutions for the purpose of acquiring, constructing, improving, maintaining, and operating "civic projects." It may borrow money and issue bonds for these purposes. It must not be confused with "taxing districts" that are subject to budgetary limitations, are endowed with taxing powers, and guided by elected directors. OBEs operate outside the governmental structure, lack taxing powers, and function under appointed directors. Except for these differences, the districts and OBEs are akin in form and function. To most politicians and officials, the latter is preferable by far because it allows them to spend and borrow without constraint, to dispense patronage without civil service restrictions, and bestow favors and benefits on special groups. An OBE is an anomaly of organization: a government entity unfettered by many statutory constraints applicable to government, a corporation without stockholders, but with a board of directors consisting of politicians or their appointees, a non-profit business that competes with business, or is protected from it as an unregulated monopoly.

The pace of off-budget activity seems to vary inversely with the imposition of tax and expenditure limitations. When tax resistance limits the scope of government revenue, politicians and bureaucrats on all levels of government learn to evade, rather than accommodate. When state and local governments chafe under constitutional restrictions, they go underground. Moreover, the federal government can be expected to encourage the move. It encourages off-budget activity by providing grants-in-aid and extending loans directly to OBEs, bypassing on-budget units of government. Aid may be given by an off-budget federal enterprise to an off-budget state or municipal enterprise with a handful of politicians and officials deciding the issue. Taxpayers have no voice in such matters.

Most government entities are spawning OBEs. There are more than ten thousand American OBEs raising funds by issuing tax-exempt bonds not subject to any legal restrictions on public debt, conducting business in competition with individual enterprise or as monopolies sheltered by legal prohibitions, and dispensing economic favors in exchange for political support. They are masquerading under various guises, such as boards, authorities, agencies, commissions, corporations, and trusts. Most of them are state and local entities; the federal government has spawned only a few, as federal spending and borrowing remain virtually unhampered by either constitutional or statutory limitations. Yet, federal off-budget financing is growing at a remarkable rate, especially through the off-budget Federal Financing Bank. Unfortunately, the American public knows little about underground government activity. In fact, there are few statistics on OBEs and the political wheeling and dealing they conceal from the public. There are few voices that warn against the consequences of such practices.

Off-Budget Local Government

During the 1960s and 1970s, local governmental bodies gave birth to thousands of independent entities that operate "off budget." On December 31, 1984, in the Commonwealth of Pennsylvania alone, some 2,548 municipal entities were pursuing 2,896 projects, most of which were off budget. Among others, there were 37 airport authorities, 121 parking authorities, 691 sewer authorities, 298 water authorities, 97 recreation authorities, 48 solid waste authorities, 82 health authorities, 95 other single-purpose authorities, and 341 multipurpose authorities. They are accustomed to borrowing between half a billion dollars and one and a half billion dollars every year and, on December 31, 1984, carried a debt of $8.2 billion.[2] Throughout the United States, an indeterminable number of municipal authorities owed a total long-term debt of $271.3 billion, of which $108 billion were "full-faith-and-credit" issues and $163.1 billion "nonguaranteed."[3]

The phenomenal growth of "off-budget" government in recent years is clearly visible in the trend from "full-faith-and-credit debt" to "nonguaranteed" indebtedness. In 1950, the former stood at $15.6 billion and the latter at $2.3 billion. In 1980, for the first time, the nonguaranteed off-budget debt exceeded the full-faith-and-credit debt ($102.1 billion versus $100.4 billion). At the end of fiscal year 1983, the ratio was $163.2 billion to $108 billion.[4] Projecting the trend, it is proper to estimate that by now (1987) the off-budget debt amounts to twice the budget debt. In short, it took some thirty years for the former to equal the latter, but only five to six years during the 1980s to soar to twice the size of full-faith-and-credit debt. In just four years (1980–1983), full-faith-and-credit debt rose $7.6 billion, but nonguaranteed debt soared by $61 billion, or eight times faster.

Politicians and government officials are reacting to tax resistance by placing government debt and expenditures off-budget, moving most of local government beyond the direct control of taxpayers. They are creating OBEs that, together with their beneficiaries, can be mobilized against all future taxpayer resistance to taxing and spending. In the meantime, they are building a pyramid of debt that is bound to place a serious financial strain on local governments nationwide.

Statewide OBEs

State governments were building their own pyramids of nonguaranteed OBE debt long before local governments joined the rush in earnest. Lawmakers and government officials on all levels of government like to spend large sums of money on popular projects, while deferring the costs through borrowing. At the state level, they succeeded in creating hundreds of statewide OBEs, which now account for more than two-thirds of all state borrowing. In terms of dollar amounts, total state long-term nonguaranteed debt now exceeds $109.6 billion while the full-faith-and-credit debt is given at $55 billion, or just 33.4 percent of the total.[5]

During the 1960s and 1970s, New York State undoubtedly paved the way for all to follow. Determined to greatly expand the state's programs in the areas of education, health care, welfare, housing, and many others, the state legislature raised taxes significantly and multiplied OBE spending. Ignoring taxpayer opposition, it launched numerous OBEs and quadrupled OBE debt, which at times amounted to some four times the guaranteed voter-approved debt. When voters rejected a $100 million housing bond issue for the third time, the legislature created the Housing Finance

Authority. The Authority issued massive amounts of nonguaranteed debt, which alone at times exceeded the total full-faith-and-credit debt of New York State. When voters rejected a $500 million higher-education bond issue for the fourth time, the legislature created the off-budget State University Construction Fund. When the voters rejected a public housing bond issue for the fifth time, the legislature reacted by creating the Urban Development Corporation. UDC was given the powers of eminent domain to override local zoning and building code controls, and to disregard any and all restrictions that hamper rapid construction. When UDC fell into default in 1975, the legislature created yet another OBE, the Project Finance Agency, which issued more OBE bonds to pay the bills of the bankrupt UDC and to cover the deficits of various other OBEs.[6] Altogether, the people of New York State were made to shoulder the heaviest debt among the fifty states, more than $27 billion as of the end of fiscal 1983.[7] More than 80 percent of this debt is off-budget, nonguaranteed, and lacking voter approval; but the creditors may rest assured: OBE bonds are "moral obligation" bonds.

Underground Federal Government

Federal politicians and officials react to taxpayer demands for fiscal restraint in the same way as local and state politicians and officials: they go underground. The Congressional Budget and Impoundment Act of 1974, which merely announced the need for fiscal discipline, without actually curbing federal spending, produced a rush to the underground. Since then, Congress has been steadily proclaiming the need for discipline and balanced budgets, but simultaneously preparing the way for placing federal spending off-budget.

The U.S. Congress uses three particular avenues of escape. First, it simply deletes numerous agencies that are federally-owned and controlled from the budget. Beginning with the Export-Import Bank, it subsequently removed the Postal Service Fund, the Rural Telephone Bank, the Rural Electrification and Telephone Revolving Fund, the Housing for the Elderly or Handicapped Fund, the Federal Financing Bank, the U.S. Railway Association, and the Pension Benefit Guaranty Corporation. More recently, it created two off-budget entities to carry out energy programs: the Synthetic Fuels Corporation and the Strategic Petroleum Reserve Account. Total off-budget outlays by these entities were estimated at $10 billion in fiscal year 1984 and $12.5 billion in fiscal 1985.[8]

A significant factor in financing federal off-budget activities is the Federal Financing Bank (FFB), which began operation in 1974. Although it is part of the Treasury Department, its transactions are excluded from the budget totals. Its lending is not counted as budget outlays, although it finances its operations by borrowing from the Treasury Department. It performs three particular off-budget functions: it purchases guaranteed loan assets from federal agencies; it disburses loan funds directly to borrowers when the loan is guaranteed by a federal agency; it lends to government agencies that are authorized to borrow from the public but almost always borrow from the FFB instead. Total net outlays of the Federal Financing Bank are estimated at $7.3 billion for fiscal year 1984 and $10.4 billion for 1985; total loans outstanding are calculated at $114.1 billion and $124.6 billion respectively.[9]

The second avenue of escape to the underground leads to a number of privately owned, but government-sponsored and controlled enterprises (GSEs). They are established to carry out government programs; they redirect credit by acting as financial intermediaries to promote greater amounts of lending to certain beneficiaries, seeking to favor lenders and borrowers especially in housing, education and agriculture. Exempt from state and local taxes, and from Securities and Exchange Commission regulations and requirements, these enterprises maintain direct lines of credit to the U.S. Treasury that range up to $4 billion.

There is the Federal Home Loan Bank System that promotes home ownership through the extension of credit to savings and other home financing institutions; the Federal Home Loan Mortgage Association that bolsters the availability of mortgage credit and liquidity in the conventional residential mortgage market; the Federal National Mortgage Association that purchases conventional and privately insured mortgages originated by mortgage bankers, savings institutions, commercial banks, and other primary lenders; the Student Loan Marketing Association that seeks to expand the amount of funds available for insured student loans; the Farm Credit System, which is a cooperative providing credit to farmers and ranchers, their cooperatives, farm-related businesses, commercial fishermen, and rural homeowners. Altogether, the government-sponsored off-budget enterprises are reported to have held $314.1 billion in loan assets in 1984, $350.1 billion in 1985, and $405.9 billion in 1986.[10] At the present rate of growth, the GSEs can be expected to achieve a trillion dollar portfolio some time in 1993.

Advancing on its third avenue of escape, making government appear smaller than it actually is or making government activity disappear altogether, the federal government is conducting over 150 loan guarantee programs that affect and redirect private funds. It guarantees the payment of the principal and interest of a loan in whole or in part in the event of default. It thus allocates economic resources by providing credit to borrowers who do not normally qualify or would have to pay higher rates. All such guarantees result in subsidies to the borrowers and significantly alter the allocation of credit. They channel private credit toward federally selected uses, which reduces the quantity of credit available to those borrowers who do not receive assistance and increases their interest costs.

Loan guarantees are not included in government outlay totals. Nevertheless, most federal functions call for credit programs that not only grant loans, but also issue loan guarantees. The loans may be off-budget, the guarantees usually are. The Federal Housing Administration (FHA) guarantees home mortgages, as does the Veterans Administration (VA). The Commodity Credit Corporation provides loan guarantees for export sales. The student loan program provides guarantees of education loans to graduate and undergraduate students. Excluding the guaranteed loans disbursed by the Federal Financing Bank and other off-budget enterprises, the total volume of guaranteed loans outstanding is estimated at $363.8 billion in 1983, and $438.8 billion in 1986. At this rate of growth, it can be expected to exceed one trillion dollars in 1994.[11]

Flexibility and Innovation

Prudent politicians and OBE officials are unlikely to admit the implications. As public servants, imbued with a sense of the public interest, they favor off-budget activities. In their hands,

OBEs are said to be more flexible, innovative, and economical than government agencies. They may even be used to circumvent voter disapproval expressed repeatedly at the ballot box.

Zeal for the public good is the characteristic of a man of honor. Yet, is it a public good to circumvent the majority decision of voters? Is it a public good to engage in off-budget activity that benefits certain interest groups at the expense of the public? Is it in the public interest that the activities undertaken by OBEs be carried out by political institutions rather than economic organizations? Is government flexibility and innovation in economic matters really a desirable feature of government, or just another term for subterfuge, waste, and arbitrariness? Even if an OBE should be more flexible, innovative, and economical than a government agency, why should it be sheltered from periodic reassessment of its performance in either the political arena or the market place?

There are two methods for the conduct of human affairs.[12] One is bureaucratic management; the other is profit management. The former is suitable and right where services have no price on the market and, therefore, cannot be tested by cost and price calculations. A police department, an army regiment, or an airforce squadron, no matter how valuable their services may be, cannot be operated as gainful enterprises. Bureaucratic management is the only method for their conduct. Profit management is the only economical method for enterprises that render services in the market place; it receives its social legitimacy from the patronage of customers who dictate the production process. Where the profit motive is the guide, business must adjust its operations to the desires of customers. Profit and loss considerations force every businessman to cater to wishes and render services the consumers deem most important. The price and cost structure guides businessmen in their task.

An OBE is an enterprise owned and operated by government. At its best, it springs from the notion that private enterprise is failing to provide a desirable service, or that it is providing it unsatisfactorily. At its worst, it serves as the private domain of politicians and officials dispensing favors to special groups, politicking with taxpayer money, building political empires, and lining their own pockets. The public may stand idly by because it may be persuaded that individual enterprise is failing to do the job. Moreover, the public may be suspicious of the profit motive, of profit management, and the private property order. Many people are anxious to substitute political action and political authority for voluntary action and consumer supremacy. They are longing for a command system.

Whatever the motivation may be, OBEs manage to escape the usual strictures and constraints under which government entities usually are forced to labor. There are regulations and controls because of the open-endedness of government expenditures. Every able manager of a government agency or enterprise knows how to improve the services of his office through additional expenditures. Every commissioner of police and commander of an army regiment or airforce squadron can use more money, as can every provost of a state university and director of a city hospital. Every manager of a municipal swimming pool or city park can improve the service to the public, provided he is granted more money. Undisturbed by profit and loss considerations, he is an eager spender of government money; however, public funds are limited, no matter how they are stretched on- and off-budget. Therefore, government must constrain and delineate the spending enthusiasm of its managers; it must proscribe many details of management; in particular, the quantity and quality of the services to be rendered, the hiring and remuneration of labor, the purchase of materials and supply, etc. In short, where profit and loss considerations do not apply or are rejected for political reasons, the only way to make managers responsible to the public is to constrain their discretion by rules and regulations.

The flexibility which OBE managers so diligently seek and pursue is the ability to escape rules and regulations. It is cleverness to escape the traditional constraints on government. It is "government unlimited" for the construction and maintenance of public housing, libraries, theaters, stadiums, airports, and zoos. OBE flexibility not only costs the people dearly, but also deceives them. After all, OBEs do not submit to any proof of effectiveness, nor do they yield to elections and referenda. They operate under no immediate constraints of consumers and no responsibility to voters. When losses are suffered, they do not cease to operate.

They pursue what they call "more important tasks," "more noble objectives," allocating funds to "worthy" and "needy" causes that differ from the orders given by customers. Economic considerations give way to "social objectives" and self-serving ends.

Winners and Losers

The "noble objectives" which its sponsors so loudly proclaim usually are economic favors to some people at the expense of others. A transportation OBE may charge a low fare that subsidizes all or some commuters. A community hospital may render services at rates that subsidize some patients at the expense of taxpayers. A city parking authority may offer "free parking" to city employees. It may do so without approval or sanction by taxpayers, who are expected to bear the deficits.

Unfortunately, the "noble objectives" may be replaced by commonplace objectives on the part of those individuals who create, manage and finance the OBEs. The altruistic motive of rendering service to the poor and underprivileged often turns to scandalous pursuit of self-interest by politicians, OBE boards and managers, employees, bankers and underwriters, attorneys, consultants, architects, engineers, and many others who profit from OBEs. The transfer benefits thus actually acrue to interested parties and promoters, leaving few benefits, but many frustrations, to the stated beneficiaries.

Politicians are the primary beneficiaries of OBEs. Fiscal limitations of any sort restrict their power to engage in transfer activity; OBEs evade the restrictions and ignore voter reluctance at the polls. By making political activity simply disappear and permitting politicians to resume spending, OBEs enable them to preach fiscal frugality on budget, while practicing political largesse off-budget.

OBEs inevitably give rise to special-interest groups that can be depended on to lend vocal support. Bankers, in particular, have a vested interest in the growth of off-budget enterprises, receiving income not only as investors in OBE projects, but also as trustees on behalf of bondholders and financial advisors to the entity. Bankers may act as underwriters of bond issues which OBEs, in contrast to government agencies, usually place on a noncompetitive basis, granting higher profit margins to underwriters. Attorneys always join the parade, acting as "bond counsels." They derive generous income from reviewing indenture specifications and issuing opinions on the deductability of bond interest from federal taxation. Their fees tend to rise with the volume of debt issued.

OBE managers and members of the board have a vested interest in OBE prosperity and growth. Appointed by a governor, mayor, or city council, *directors* have ample latitude to pursue their own self-interest. They may engage in business activities that directly supplement that of the OBE. They may speculate in real estate in anticipation of OBE activity. They may manipulate OBE contracts or place supporters in patronage positions. At the least, they may guide OBE dealings in such a way that friendly politicians and their supporters derive some benefit from the enterprise. OBE *managers*, who direct the day-to-day operations, usually operate in secrecy and undisturbed by audits by the government entity that created them. Surely, they are always mindful of the politicians who created them and, therefore, are quick to accommodate political pressures by providing patronage positions. If an OBE succeeds in generating revenue to cover its operating costs and debt service, and thus manages to be financially independent, the excess revenue is held internally to be used by management. OBEs pay no taxes or license fees, post no performance bonds, face little paperwork and regulatory tape that strangle individual enterprises. They pay no dividends to the sponsoring unit of government, but usually earn enough to grant generous fringe benefits to managers and employees.

When OBEs fail to cover their costs, taxpayers must brace for a summons. The number of OBE bankruptcies is rather small because politicians cannot afford to let their projects fail and their artifices become visible. They are quick to use tax revenues to provide government subsidies and grants to avoid default. Although there is no explicit commitment for government to come to the rescue, there is what politicians call a "moral commitment" to cover a shortfall. It serves to reassure investors who are urged to buy the bonds. Judging from the ready acceptance of OBE obligations, American bankers and other institutional investors continue to be reassured by such "moral commitments."

Taxpayers, in one form or another, must bear the cost of OBE loss and failure. Yet, even when OBEs manage to operate in the black, they crowd out competing borrowers and allocate capital and labor to political uses, rather than economic employment. They withdraw scarce economic resources from urgent want satisfaction so that political interests may be served, and channel capital from more productive to less productive employment, which depresses labor productivity and lowers labor income. No matter how efficient an OBE may be, it amounts to malinvestment and maladjustment because it is a creation of politics. After all, if an economic project is economical and profitable because consumers patronize it, it is readily pursued and realized by individual enterprises. If businessmen shun it and investors avoid it, but politicians discover it or interested parties urge politicians to embark upon it, it is likely to be uneconomical.

A few OBEs are said to be highly profitable, which may permit their managers to embark upon other economic activities. Toll road and bridge authorities may be very profitable, charging whatever the traffic will bear. The Port Authority of New York, for instance, is using its control over airports, bridges, toll roads, and harbor facilities to build a vast business empire. Some of its revenue constitutes monopolistic gain that enriches the Port Authority and its dependents at the expense of the public. It always leads to poor service and breeds political corruption. Even in service, honor and integrity, a profitable OBE is a malformation that rests on political privilege. Exempted from taxes or license fees, and protected by regulation and restriction, it serves "higher ends" which are uneconomical ends. It receives its legitimacy from political power rather than the patronage of customers.

Industrial Development Agencies

The businessman's "special" is the industrial development agency (IDA) that issues tax-exempt industrial revenue bonds (IRBs) and finances favorite private enterprises. IDAs are the fastest growing type of all the OBEs and are estimated to exceed $10 billion in annual bond sales. Most of them issue obligations without the "full-faith-and-credit" of the sponsoring government; their operations are off-budget and beyond the reach of voters and taxpayers. Their obligations are nonguaranteed, that is, they depend on the credit of the private borrower and the revenue from the development project. If the project fails, the bondholders bear the loss. If it stays alive, the private borrower pockets the difference between the tax-exempt rate and the market rate of interest. He is enjoying a privilege that is created and bestowed by politicians.

The friends of IDAs are quick to point out that the agencies are instrumental in providing financial resources to private firms, especially small businesses, that they facilitate production where there would be none otherwise, that they raise productivity and reduce unemployment. IDAs are said to confer a "public benefit" through the development of commerce and industry, and the promotion of the general welfare. Of course, such rhetoric builds on the assumption that private fincancial institutions are failing to provide the necessary resources to many firms, especially small businesses, that private lenders fail to encourage production where it is needed, and that they do not raise productivity and do not reduce unemployment. IDA rhetoric tacitly assumes that private enterprises do not confer a "public benefit" and do not promote the general welfare.

Unfortunately, the rhetoric differs from reality. Every businessman enjoying customer patronage, whether he be a baker, banker, or barber is conferring a public benefit, raising production, and reducing unemployment; businessmen earn their livelihood by producing products and rendering services wherever they are needed. Countless entrepreneurs are forever searching for new opportunities to embark upon needed production. If they find none, it is likely that no economic opportunity exists. If politicians discover one, that is, attorneys, accountants, and college professors wearing political hats, and special interests applaud it, the project is likely to be a transfer scheme that benefits some people at the expense of others. Transfer allocation replaces market allocation, serving political interests that are contrary to the interests of the general public.

IDAs are known to assist ailing and failing businesses that either are losing the patronage of customers or making inefficient use of their resources. In both cases, IDAs not only countermand consumer sovereignty, that is, public interest and control, but also promote economic inefficiency and incompetence. Moreover, by granting tax exemptions to special-interest groups, IDAs create vocal groups of grateful supporters who can be depended upon to defend and promote IDAs and the use of IRBs. Small businesses are not one of them; they are the least likely recipients of IDA largesse because their voices may not be audible in the noise of the corporate clamor for privilege. Giant corporations that have the labor power to deal with numerous IDAs, that enjoy expert legal assistance and command political clout are the primary beneficiaries of IRB financing. Large manufacturing and retailing firms make extensive use of IRBs to finance expansion projects. In fact, because McDonald's Corporation financed the construction of hundreds of new restaurants with IRBs, the street calls all IDA obligations "burger bonds" and their beneficiaries "burger debtors." Obviously, "burger bonds" are instrumental in destroying countless small enterprises that cannot compete with subsidized McDonald's restaurants or K-Mart stores. The voices of the businesses that perished as a result of burger-bond favors are no longer audible, but the voices of the giant corporations, investment bankers, and law firms that benefit from IRB sales are heard clearly in the chorus of special interests.

The net effect of IRB financing is a gross distortion of American business and outright waste of productive funds. IDA projects inflict revenue losses on governmental treasuries, and lead to rising interest rates and higher borrowing costs for all borrowers, public and private. Above all, they call for further politicalization of economic life. On all levels, government, party politicians, and government officials now sit in judgment of economic phenomena. Local politicians adjudge the need of a project and adjudicate the benefits to be bestowed. Federal officials, by offering or withdrawing federal tax exemption, hold veto power over them all. The Revenue Expenditure and Control Act of 1968 provides the legal setting; it withdrew tax exemption from all IDAs except those financing air and water pollution control equipment, airports, docks, wharves, electricity, gas and water services, industrial parks, parking, mass transportation, housing, sewage, sports facilities, and trade shows and convention centers. The act offers tax exemption to all issues not exceeding \$5 million to finance plants and equipment for industrial facilities, which was later raised to \$10 million.[13] It is obvious that American economic life is molded and guided by such powerful directives; however, it is neither efficient nor equitable to grant tax relief to some businesses and withhold it from others.

Political power intoxicates the best hearts. No man is wise enough, nor good enough, to be trusted with much political power. Constitutional government is built on this very knowledge; it is cogent evidence of the distrust of human beings in political power. It rests on a deep conviction that individuals vested with authority must be restrained by something more than their own discretion: by bills of rights, laws, rules, regulations, and mandates by the people they govern.

Off-budget government escapes most such restraints and opens the gates of political power. It escapes the constraints because changing thoughts and values are either moderating the common distrust of political power, or the distrust is failing to restrain the growing powers of government. The deep conviction that government must be restrained is giving way to the belief that government must be able to engage in economic activity as its agents see fit. It is yielding to the ancient notion that political rulers are endowed with extraordinary powers. Unfortunately, they are not. Yet, they are always eager to ignore the traditional constraints and follow their own caprice.

5

DEFICITS DO MATTER

Private vs. Government Debt

To secure the revenue it deems necessary for defraying its various expenses, modern government relies primarily on three sources of revenue: taxation, inflation, and borrowing. The usual source is *taxation*, a compulsory exaction from taxpayers who suffer reductions in income so that government may engage in its activities. A popular means is *inflation*, which is the act of inflating the available currency and credit by the government money monopoly, endowed with legal-tender power. The basic nature of inflation is akin to taxation, although its effects reach far beyond the sphere of fiscal finances. *Borrowing*, finally, is an alternative means of securing revenue to cover government expenditures. In contrast to taxation and inflation, borrowing may secure funds on a voluntary exchange basis. Private individuals voluntarily purchase government securities that pledge interest income and repayment of the capital in the future. This traditional distinction has become rather obscure in recent years, as government no longer relies completely on voluntary lending, but also coerces private financial institutions, which it regulates, to purchase its obligations. Even the pledge of repayment can no longer be taken seriously, as new debt is added every day, and the mountain of debt surpasses all possibilities of repayment. All three methods of government finance reduce the real wealth of private individuals.

Most individuals are mindful of the future and, therefore, tend to be savers. Whether or not their savings lead to capital formulation and economic improvements depends on the employment of the funds saved. In an unhampered capital market, the savings may be deposited with banks or other financial institutions that lend them to qualified borrowers. In search of interest income and capital safety, banks tend to invest the deposits productively; they finance capital investments that expand or modernize the apparatus of production. Saving and investing thus bring about a rise in the marginal productivity of labor, and not only raise wage rates, but also provide an interest to the saver and investor.

Government debt differs fundamentally from private debt. While the latter is generally productive and indicative of capital formation and economic improvement, the former is primarily consumptive. Throughout history, there is not a single example of capital accumulation by government. It always uses the savings of its subjects, and mostly consumes them, financing expensive wars, building pyramids and temples of politics, or bestowing benefits on the social classes in power. Even where government invests the funds in the construction of roads and other public works, it usually invests them serving lesser needs than they would have served in the hands of the savers.

Private and federal debt differ in yet another important respect. The federal government possesses powers of money creation which individuals and local governments do not have. The power over a monopolistic central bank with legal tender power allows government to suffer budget deficits without exacting more funds from taxpayers or calling upon investors to purchase its obligations. The power to create money may even allow it to generate budgetary deficits without, at the same time, increasing its debt. The Treasury "borrows" from the Federal Reserve, which is disguised money creation. It issues legal-tender money, deprives its subjects of economic resources, and incurs no net debt. The effects are quite different from genuine debt issue.[1]

Measurements of Debt

The instruments of federal debt, whether they are Treasury bills, notes, or bonds are written promises to pay the holder a sum of money at a certain time at a stated rate of interest. They are promises made in exchange for the individual savings placed at the disposal of government. The total volume of debt is a fair indicator of the activity of government and the magnitude of individual savings consumed by government.

Government debt may be measured in units of the national currency; however, in this age of fiat money, the monetary unit is depreciating, which renders comparisons over time and among several governmental units rather dubious. To arrive at more meaningful comparisons, calculations would need to be adjusted, using multipliers, to arrive at the current price which a government obligation would have to approximate to reflect the real purchasing power it had on the day of issue. Such calculations become rather complex and controversial, given the uncertainty of goods prices in the past. For purposes of comparisons, macro-economists are inclined to determine the ratio of total debt to gross national or gross domestic product, or the ratio of new debt to total individual savings, all of which run aground on the futility of holistic thinking. This essay points at the magnitude of federal debt in terms of U.S. dollars from the beginning of the republic until today.

Growth of Federal Debt
(in millions of U.S. dollars)

Year	Dollars	Year	Dollars	Year	Dollars
1791	75	1865	2,678	1925	20,516
1802	81	1870	2,436	1930	16,185
1815	100	1875	2,156	1935	28,701
1820	91	1880	2,091	1940	42,968
1825	84	1885	1,579	1945	258,682
1830	49	1890	1,122	1950	257,377
1835	0	1895	1,097	1955	274,418
1840	4	1900	1,263	1960	284,700
1845	16	1905	1,132	1965	313,819
1850	63	1910	1,147	1970	370,094
1855	36	1915	1,191	1975	533,189
1860	65	1920	24,299	1980	914,300
				1985	1,827,500
				5/8/1987	2,255,893

Source: Data from 1791 to 1850 taken from *Annual Report of the Secretary of the Treasury on the State of the Finances* for the Fiscal Year Ended June 30, 1903, p. 63; from 1855 to 1935 from *ibid.*, pp. 562–563. Recent years taken from *Treasury Bulletins* and *Annual Reports*.

Official debt statistics only reveal what the government has borrowed in the past and is obligated to repay. They do not show the tremendous volume of obligations the federal government has undertaken and is bound to face in the future. If these obligations are included in the debt picture, the totals become even larger. They would be larger yet, if the debt of state and local governments, as well as off-budget government authorities, were to be included.

Every year the National Taxpayers Union releases its estimate of the total federal debt, liabilities, and obligations. As of early 1986, the total exceeded $13 trillion.

Debt or Liability Item	Federal Obligations (in millions)
Public Debt	$2,078,700
Accounts Payable	235,652
Undelivered Orders	560,043
Long Term Contracts	13,563
Loan and Credit Guarantees	662,244
Insurance Commitments	2,659,067
Annuity Programs	6,892,000
Unadjudicated Claims	37,639
Foreign Development Banks	12,807
Other Contingencies	22,940
TOTAL Federal Obligations	**$13,174,655**

Source: *Dollars & Sense*, Vol. 17, No. 2, March 1986, p. 5.

The obligational debt becomes real debt when the obligations fall due. They may not appear in the budget, which explains the difference between the annual budget deficits as calculated by the U.S. Treasury and the annual rise in federal debt. The latter usually is 30–40 percent higher than the former. In a *Fortune* article (May 12, 1986), Duane R. Kullberg estimated that the federal debt, when calculated on an accrual basis, rather than cash basis, stood at $3.8 trillion, rather than just $2.125 trillion.

In the fall of 1972, this writer estimated and projected the trend of official federal deficits and debt in a study titled *Inflation or Gold Standard?* (Lansing, MI: a Bramble Minibook, March 1973).

His calculations rested on a number of assumptions that have proven to be fairly accurate over the years. The final verdict can be rendered in the year 2003.

The Federal Budget and Debt
(In millions of dollars)

	Receipts	Expend- itures	Surplus or Deficit	Public Debt at End of Year
1933	1,997	4,598	-2,602	22,539
1943	25,097	78,909	-53,812	140,796
1953	71,495	76,769	-5,274	266,123
1963	106,560	111,311	-4,751	310,800
1973 estimated	224,984	249,796	-24,812	473,300
1973 actual	**232,225**	**246,526**	**-14,301**	**468,400**
1983 projected	700,000	825,000	-125,000	1,400,000
1983 actual	**600,562**	**808,327**	**-207,764**	**1,381,900**
1993 projected	3,000,000	4,000,000	-1,000,000	4,000,000
2003 projected in new currency	300,000	300,000	0	1,000,000

Source of 1933–1973 data: *The Budget of the United States Government*, 1974, pp. 370, 371. Projections by writer.

Historically, the large increases in federal debt occurred during war emergencies, when governments felt free to engage in deficit financing. Under the influence of "the new economics" and "the entitlement ideology," the U.S. government as well as governments the world over now resort to deficit financing on a regular basis. Some consume all the savings coming to market and even deplete the capital stock accumulated in the past.

We Owe It to Ourselves

The champions of government spending are telling us that government debt does not matter; after all, we owe it to ourselves. As long as government borrows funds internally and expenditures are financed from internal sources, so the notion goes, no real cost is incurred. Interest payment on debt merely represents transfers from taxpayers to bondholders. Debt to foreigners, by contrast, is seen as a wholly different matter because it necessitates interest payments to outsiders. It is analogous to private debt.[2]

"We owe it to ourselves," this notion seems to spring always anew. It was very popular with European monarchs during the sixteenth, seventeenth and eighteenth centuries because it placed them in the center of economic life and made them the promoters and guardians of national prosperity. Kings and princes who looked upon the economic lives of their subjects as mere extensions of their own economic activities viewed their debts as both accounts payable and accounts receivable. After all, if the subjects belong to his lordship, their property is also his. The debt he may owe them he owes to himself.

The so-called Keynesian revolution during the late 1930s revived the doctrine and promoted it to a great principle of economic knowledge. Economists throughout the Western world accepted it almost universally. Yet, it is as fallacious today as it was when the kings and their ministers proclaimed it. It is the rationale of spendthrift governments, eager to spend more money than they have.

The federal government debt now exceeds $2 trillion and is expected to reach the $3 trillion mark by the end of the decade. We do not owe these sums to ourselves; the U.S. government owes them to individual savers and investors. The "now-generation" that consumes the savings creates debt obligations and expects future generations to pay them. At first, it may consume only a small share of the individual savings coming to market, causing a slow-down in capital formation and economic development. In time, the share consumed by its apparatus of politics tends to grow until it depletes all savings and causes economic progress to grind to a halt. In a final frenzy of spending, it may actually consume capital accumulated by previous generations, and thus cause economic conditions to deteriorate. For the benefit of its favorite beneficiaries and an army of civil servants and politicians, the now-generation may consume the patrimony of its forebears, and place a crushing burden of debt on its descendents.

During the 1980s, the federal government borrowed enormous amounts from foreigners. Between 1980 and 1986, it placed some $90 billion of its obligations in foreign hands, which was as much as it borrowed from foreigners during the entire period from 1965 to 1979, a period three times as long. By the end of 1986, it owed foreigners some $210.2 billion and was paying them an annual interest of $21.2 billion.[3] Actually, foreigners not only lent the U.S. government money that facilitated the budget deficits, but they also financed the trade deficits.

Debts are Tax Liens

Deficits and debts signal future tax exactions. Having incurred the debt in the past, government, in order to repay the funds or just to pay the interest, must levy taxes in the future. In essence, therefore, a government debt is a government claim against personal income and private property—an unpaid tax bill so to speak—that will fall due in the future.[4] It is bound to depress labor productivity and the value of productive property. To ignore the claim is to ignore the future.

To most people, government spending is a panacea for economic evils and difficulties, a cure-all for human woes. Where progress and prosperity give way to economic stagnation, government is expected to stimulate through deficit spending. Where there is unemployment, government is expected to supplement private demand and thus create jobs; where there is poverty, it is expected to provide affluence through more spending and debt. Yet, as government has no source of wealth other than that which it exacts from its citizenry, it can distribute only that which it exacts. It can provide benefits only by imposing burdens and raising costs. It can incur budget deficits only by imposing new burdens on future taxpayers.

Government cannot pile up debt without ever paying it off; all government indebtedness must ultimately be paid off with tax revenues, or be repudiated. Repudiation in any shape or disguise is merely another form of taxation. When seen in this light, the supposed benefits of deficit spending appear as painful exactions from hapless taxpayers. To build a pyramid of federal debt to finance the benefits is to delay the exactions and pay interest on the delay.

The desire to delay the inevitable may or may not be related to the purposes of spending. The deficit spenders are quick to point to the temporal pattern of benefits that are expected to flow from the spending. If the spending is anticipated to yield benefits over a period of time, they contend, considerations of efficiency and equity suggest that the spending be financed by loans. Yet, such reasoning is likely to ignore the fact that the beneficiaries of the government projects that render long-lasting benefits may not be the same as the victims who are expected to finance the projects. The harbor or highway to be built may benefit a few users, while the costs are imposed on future taxpayers throughout the country. Moreover, the government projects may not even pass the test of the market; the costs may exceed the benefits, imposing greater financial burdens on taxpayers than the users are reaping in benefits. On net balance, the government projects may actually consume economic resources and render future taxes ever more onerous.

Historically, wars and preparations for war have created mountains of government debt. Public opinion has always sanctioned such debt. Yet, public approval does not negate the fact that war expenditures consume economic resources en masse, deplete the capital market, and visibly impoverish society. They render future taxation more onerous.

Deficits Breed Inflation

Taxing is an easy business. In the words of Edmund Burke, "any projector can contrive new impositions; any bungler can add to the old; but is it altogether wise to have no other bounds to your impositions than the patience of those who are to bear them?" The transfer society is forever testing the bounds of patience of taxpayers. Having reached the limit and still facing loud demands for more benefits, it is tempted to resort to deficit financing.

Economists draw a distinction between financing which results in debt because of a present deficiency in income or overspending, and financing which is intended to result in debt as a means of control, called "functional finance" and "compensatory finance." The huge federal deficits in recent years sprang from a combination of both.

Both types of deficit financing are inflationary, causing the purchasing power of the monetary unit to fall and goods prices to rise. Yet, the rate of inflation may differ greatly depending on the sources of financing: the people's savings or the government printing presses. The former consumes productive capital, depresses economic output, and causes painful readjustments with generally rising prices; the latter calls for "monetization of debt." This is the process by which the federal debt is used to increase the stock of money and credit. Essentially, it is carried out through the purchase of government obligations by the Federal Reserve System, forcing Federal Reserve notes on the public.

Both sources of funds are tapped to cover the annual deficits. Yet, the monetary authorities may vary the rate at which they are using each of the sources. For a few years, they may rely primarily on the capital markets, consuming the people's savings en masse until the detrimental effects are painfully felt, at which time they may return to their printing presses. When the evil consequences of debt monetarization become clearly visible, they may return to the former, or seek to strike a precarious balance between the two. Deficit financing, no matter what sources of funds it may tap, is highly unstable because every one of its sources leads to increasingly undesirable consequences.

The most popular method of deficit financing is the issue of legal-tender money by the money monopoly. It not only facilitates deficit spending, but also reduces interest costs to zero. Surely, the U.S. Treasury pays interest on all its obligations, including those owned by the Federal Reserve, but all such funds are promptly returned as "miscellaneous receipts." Because of the interest savings alone, government authorities prefer monetization of debt to the consumption of savings, on which interest needs to be paid. Anyway, as the national economy grows, so they argue, government has to provide an increasing stock of money "to maintain a constant level of product and service prices."

This old doctrine of the desirability of a stable price level through monetary management, to which nearly all contemporary economists adhere, has given birth to the doctrine of aggregate-demand manipulation, which, in the garb of Keynesian economics, has conquered the economic world. Debt management and the monetization of the federal debt now serve as macroeconomic tools in promoting economic stability and growth. By mandate of the Employment Act of 1946, which legalized Keynesian thought and policy, the federal government now expends funds for purposes of economic prosperity and full employment. The state of the budget is of no importance.

Keynesian economics fundamentally disagrees with classical economics in holding that the private-property order tends to sink into depression and unemployment. The remedy advocated in one form or another is deficit spending and money creation. In stagnation and decline, the monetary authorities are called upon to "stimulate," "bolster," and "revive" the national economy. Every administration from Roosevelt to Reagan has labored diligently and spent freely to achieve these objectives. Keynesian economists frequently call for "infusions of aggregate demand" because unemployment continues to haunt some seven to eight million Americans, and the rate of "economic growth" proves to be embarrassingly low. Yet, they, too, conclude that budget deficits should be avoided as the economy approaches full employment. Federal deficits are believed to be appropriate for recessions; they are said to be inflationary at other times. If they are already very large at the beginning of a recession, public policy makers may be reluctant to pursue yet larger deficits during the recession. They may be reluctant to prescribe Keynesian remedies which, according to Keynesians, would make recessions deeper and larger than they otherwise would be.

One may disagree completely with the Keynesian rationale, and yet agree with the conclusion that government budgets should be balanced. In fact, they should be balanced all the time, not just during periods of full employment, which may be slow in coming. Government deficits consume economic substance and wealth; by their very nature, they depress economic activity. The stimulation that may be observed in the wake of deficit spending is the result of willful currency and credit creation; it is the effect of the injection of monetary funds that lower interest rates and misguide businessmen in their investment decisions. When interest rates are lower than market rates, and goods prices are made to rise faster than wage rates and fringe costs, the demand for labor tends to rise and unemployment may fall. This morsel of economic knowledge constitutes the secret ingredient of the Keynesian recipe.

Deficit spending during a recession is destined to fail whenever goods prices fail to rise faster than labor costs. Workers and their trade unions may see through the inflation machination and readjust their demands to the willful depreciation, demanding cost-of-living clauses and other compensation adjustments[5] to offset their losses. When the workers no longer can be made to suffer reductions in real income, the Keynesian recipe loses its power. Moreover, when administered in massive doses during recessions, after large deficits were suffered during the preceding booms, deficit spending may turn into runaway inflation with a deep depression and mass unemployment. A twenty percent inflation rate may cause a twenty percent unemployment rate because production capital may no longer function; it may join other assets in the flight into inflation hedges.

Deficit spending is the mother of debt, which is the mother of folly and crime. A small debt may be cleared off in a little time, whereas a large debt may never be repaid. A debtor who owes a great deal may despair of ever being able to pay and, therefore, be susceptible to the temptations of default. The U.S. government owes two trillion dollars, and more every day.

Politicians and officials in high places are pointing to the fact that the federal debt has actually declined in terms of purchasing power, as well as relative value. They are supported by "supply-side" economists who point to the shrinkage of debt. They all are convinced that federal deficits no longer matter.[6]

It is true, the federal debt has actually declined, both in purchasing power and relative value. Yet, this decline in itself is a great evil that is spawning many other evils. Most of it is the handiwork of inflation, the willful policy of currency debauchery, that enriches one class of people at the expense of another. It deprives creditors of their rightful claims, and enriches the debtors, primarily politicians and government officials who incur the debt. It breeds economic and political conflict as it pits the economic interests of one social class against another, jeopardizing peaceful social cooperation and endangering the democratic process. Surely, debt and depreciation do matter.

Depreciation of debt by inflation is repudiation, pure and simple, the refusal to acknowledge an undiminished debt. It is deceit, wicked and desperate; its consequences can never be foreseen. When deceit has been practiced in matters where all should be fair, confidence cannot be easily restored. In financial terms, interest rates signal the dangers of repudiation; they cannot be expected to return to normal as long as deceit can be expected. In this sense, the deceiver is bound to pay a price for his evil ways.

The rising burden of interest on the federal debt is illustrating the point. In fiscal year 1986, the U.S. government is estimated to pay $196.095 billion on its debt; in 1987, it is scheduled to pay $206.855 billion.[7] In terms of federal revenue, the interest is expected to consume some twenty-five percent of estimated receipts, in terms of gross national product, some 4.5 percent, which is the highest in U.S. history. Even in 1945, when the federal debt amounted to 133 percent of GNP, the burden of interest consumed less than ten percent of net receipts and barely two percent of GNP. If government expenditures on goods and services were deleted from GNP because government revenue merely consists of exactions from private production, the interest burden on every American would loom even greater. Surely, debt and interest do matter.

Balance-of-Payments Deficits

It is ironic that many federal spenders are lamenting the U.S. trade deficits, and pointing in all directions, while they themselves are the primary cause of the deficits. Concerned about the difference in dollars between American purchases abroad and American sales to foreigners, they exert increasing pressure for trade restrictions, for raising taxes, boosting spending, or just for imposing limits on the quantity and quality of foreign goods which Americans are permitted to buy. They cite a variety of reasons why they should impose new restrictions or impose new taxes, all of which would make matters worse.

The balance-of-trade concern is a new offshoot of sixteenth and seventeenth century Mercantilistic thought. Yet, while the Mercantilists explained the loss of gold as a deplorable consequence of balance-of-trade deficits, contemporary Mercantilists point at depressions and unemployment as the major consequence. Unpatriotic speculators and investors are said to take their money abroad, develop efficient foreign facilities of production, and then export their output to the United States. Massive shipments inflict losses on domestic industries and cause the loss of many American jobs.

The fallacies of these ancient notions in modern garb are clearly visible. The movement of money across international borders does not differ from any movement across state or city lines, from New York to New Jersey, or New York City to Jersey City. Money does not move as a result of favorable or unfavorable balances of payment; imbalances are the effect of deliberate changes in cash holdings on the part of the people in both countries. If the people in one country would not want to reduce their cash holdings and the people in another country would not want to increase theirs, there could be no payment surpluses or deficits.

Large American trade deficits are the consequence of individual choices at home and abroad. Yet, these choices, which differ from person to person and tend to neutralize one another, may be affected by policies and conditions created by the apparatus of politics. Since 1971, three particular government interventions have exerted their influence on the people's choices:

1. Suspension of gold payments by President Nixon on August 15, 1971, which placed the U.S. dollar in the center of the world monetary order, created a world-wide demand for U.S. dollars. If this had been the only factor of change, the outflow of dollars into individual cash holdings all over the world would have lowered goods prices in the United States, which in time would have arrested the outflow of U.S. dollars and restored the balance. Unfortunately, U.S. monetary authorities embarked upon massive currency and credit expansion, which generated massive balance-of-payment deficits until the dollar crises of 1978 and 1979 called a temporary halt to the dollar flow.

2. Where governments engage in currency and credit expansion, the people may react by reducing their cash holdings. Throughout the 1970s, and again since the fall of 1982, the United States has led the way to easy money and credit. Giant budget deficits brought forth gigantic Federal Reserve credit expansion to facilitate those deficits. In reaction, Amer-

icans in all walks of life, from corporate directors to eager housewives, were intent upon reducing the amount of money held and upon buying goods instead. They bought American as well as foreign products. They imported whatever they could not find at home and what they could buy abroad at bargain prices. With every new spin of the dollar printing presses, the U.S. balance of payments turned more "unfavorable."

The U.S. balance-of-payments deficits are the consequence of the large budget deficits. Unfortunately, rather than eliminate the cause of the deficits by balancing the budget, the Administration and the Congress are searching for ways to restrict imports. Instead of retreating from previous intervention, they prefer to advance another step toward political regulation and control.

3. The massive budget deficits signal substantial capital consumption. In a country with high savings rates, a budget deficit that consumes some five percent of national income merely reduces the rate of development. In the United States, where the savings rate tends to be rather low, the budget deficit may actually consume most savings, and thus cause economic expansion to grind to a halt. They cause interest rates to be higher than they otherwise would, which inflicts grief and hardship on capital-intensive industries. As interest rates rise, these industries are forced to contract. In competition with Toyota Corporation, which may pay six percent on its capital improvements, General Motors Corporation paying twelve percent may no longer be competitive and, therefore, be forced to contract.

    The contraction of capital-intensive industries as a result of the federal budget deficits necessitates readjustments in the balance of payments. Instead of exporting industrial products, the American people will offer their services in the world market in exchange for the products they import; or they may exchange their real property, their corporations, banks, hotels, farms, and office buildings for industrial products made in capital-intensive countries. They may market their IOUs wherever foreign investors are willing to buy them.

If foreign investors should ever conclude that they have enough dollar liquidity and enough investments in the United States, the dollar must fall. In fact, it may plummet when foreigners lose confidence in U.S. economic and monetary policy, when willful dollar depreciation inflicts painful losses on their dollar investments, and causes them to liquidate rather than invest. When foreigners become dollar sellers rather than dollar buyers, the international situation is bound to change. The American dollar will fall, the flood of imports will cease, and goods prices will soar. In the end, large federal deficits are bound to generate serious inflation pressure.

Real Income is Falling

Transfer policies favor present consumption at the expense of the future. A huge government debt signals huge consumption of economic resources for political ends, incurred in the past at the expense of the future. It speaks of factories not built, stores not opened, businesses not started, and jobs not created.

Deficits consume funds that otherwise would be available for private investment; they represent a direct transfer from investment to consumption. The deficits of the U.S. government, resulting primarily from expenditures for national defense, Social Security, Medicare, and a myriad of other transfer programs, curtail the rate of expansion, keep productivity and labor income lower than they otherwise would be, impede international competitiveness, and cause American levels of living to fall, relative to those in other countries where people save and invest more.

It may be argued that other governments throughout the world incur similar deficits and, therefore, exert similarly restrictive effects on their countries. Such an argument is badly misleading because the savings rate is much higher in many other countries. Where the investment rate exceeds twenty to thirty percent of income, the impact of a five percent deficit is less adverse on investment than in the United States where the savings rate barely reaches five percent. Americans cannot afford any further reduction in investment through government deficits.

The levels of living of most Americans are falling. According to the 1987 Economic Report of the President, weekly earnings, measured in 1977 dollars, have fallen almost continually during the past fifteen years. In December 1986, they stood at $170.30; they amounted to $172.16 in 1962. According to the Report, working Americans have suffered a decline of some fourteen percent since 1972, when weekly earnings reached an all-time high of $198.41. The decline to present levels is actually steeper than indicated because the official statistics do not reveal the rising burden of taxation by all levels of government. Inflation has pushed wage earners into higher tax brackets, which, together with deficit spending, has allowed government to exact an ever larger share of income. If politicians, government officials, and transfer beneficiaries were deleted from the income statistics, the earnings of victims alone would have fallen significantly. Moreover, the present level of weekly earnings, no matter how low it may be, is bolstered by massive foreign lending. As soon as the balance of trade deficits, most of which constitute foreign lending, come to a halt, American levels of living are destined to plummet further. Of course, in current dollars, income levels continue to rise, which misleads many Americans into believing that they are better off. The decline thus continues, while politicians, government officials, and their beneficiaries eagerly reassure their victims that they, too, are better off.

Average Gross Weekly Earnings
In Private Nonagricultural Industries
(1970–1986)

Year or Month	Current Dollars	1977 Dollars	Percent Changes from a Year Earlier	
			Current Dollars	1977 Dollars
1970	119.83	186.94	4.6	− 1.3
1971	127.31	190.58	6.2	1.9
1972	136.90	198.41	7.5	4.1
1973	145.39	198.35	6.2	0
1974	154.76	190.12	6.4	− 4.1
1975	163.53	184.16	5.7	− 3.1
1976	175.45	186.85	7.3	1.5
1977	189.00	189.00	7.7	1.2
1978	203.70	189.31	7.8	.2

Year or Month	Current Dollars	1977 Dollars	Percent Changes from a Year Earlier	
			Current Dollars	1977 Dollars
1979	219.91	183.41	8.0	− 3.1
1980	235.10	172.74	6.9	− 5.8
1981	255.20	170.13	8.5	− 1.5
1982	267.26	168.09	4.7	− 1.2
1983	280.70	171.26	5.0	1.9
1984	292.86	172.78	4.3	.9
1985	299.09	170.42	2.1	− 1.4
1986	304.85	171.07	1.9	.4
1985: Jan.	295.40	171.15	2.0	− 1.2
Feb.	295.95	170.97	2.1	− 1.3
Mar.	297.50	171.08	2.7	− 1.2
Apr.	297.35	170.30	1.4	− 2.6
May	298.55	170.80	2.4	− 1.5
June	299.09	170.62	2.6	− 1.5
July	297.54	169.44	1.5	− 2.2
Aug.	299.79	170.43	2.3	−.6
Sept.	300.84	170.74	2.1	−.6
Oct.	301.19	170.45	2.7	−.2
Nov.	301.02	169.49	2.3	− 1.1
Dec.	303.63	170.20	2.5	− 1.1
1986: Jan.	303.80	169.72	3.1	−.6
Feb.	303.98	170.58	2.5	−.5
Mar.	304.68	171.94	2.4	.4
Apr.	303.46	171.93	2.1	.9
May	303.80	171.83	1.9	.7
June	303.28	170.67	1.1	−.2
July	302.93	170.57	1.7	.5
Aug.	305.20	171.46	1.8	.6
Sept.	303.97	170.49	1.0	−.3
Oct.	305.36	170.78	1.4	.2
Nov.	307.98	171.86	2.0	1.1
Dec.	305.86	170.30	.7	.1

Source: Economic Report of the President, 1987, p. 293.

6

WORSE THAN 1929

Then and Now

History is a distinct product of man's spiritual nature, an expression of his thought and understanding. It is explanation and interpretation of the successes and achievements, follies and misfortunes of mankind; it is teaching by example and by warning. Unfortunately, man rarely learns from history; his interests and passions, fears and resentments tend to smother the lessons.

The reader who seeks to learn from economic history cannot help but be alarmed about the great similarities between the financial policies and events preceding the 1929 stock market crash and the policies conducted today. He may conclude that, in time, present policies must have similarly disastrous effects as those of the 1920s. If the monetary policies of the 1920s brought forth the Great Depression, similar policies during the 1980s are likely to produce another depression.

Although the Great Depression engulfed the world economy more than fifty years ago, it lives on in the memories of the living generations. It lives on as a nightmare with those individuals old enough to remember, and as a frightening specter in the textbooks of our youth. In fact, its indelible imprints are visible not only in the political and economic thoughts of most Americans, but also in the economic policies that affect their daily lives.

The spectacular crash of 1929 followed five years of intermittent credit expansion by the Federal Reserve System under the Coolidge Administration. It all started in 1924, when, after a sharp decline in business, the Reserve banks suddenly created some $500 million in new credit, which led to a bank credit expansion of over $4 billion in less than one year. While the immediate effects of this new powerful expansion of the nation's money and credit were seemingly beneficial, initiating a new economic boom and effacing the 1924 decline, the ultimate outcome was most disastrous. It was the beginning of a monetary policy that led to the stock market crash in 1929, and to the following depression. In fact, the expansion of Federal Reserve credit in 1924 constituted what Benjamin Anderson, in his great treatise on recent economic history, *Economics and the Public Welfare*, called "the beginning of the New Deal."[1]

For the same reason, the Federal Reserve System launched yet another burst of inflation in 1927 that lasted through 1928. Some $400 million in new Federal Reserve credit were created, discount rates reduced, and bank credit expansion invited. Consequently, total currency outside banks, and demand and time deposits in the United States increased from $44.51 billion at the end of June, 1924, to $52.23 billion in 1927, and $55.17 billion in 1929. The expansion of money and credit was accompanied by rapidly rising real estate and stock prices. According to Standard & Poor's common stock index, the prices for industrial securities rose from 59.4 in June of 1922, to 103.4 in June of 1927, and 195.2 in September of 1929. Railroad stocks climbed from 189.2 to 316.2, and 446.0 respectively. During the same period, the public utilities rose from 82 to 135.1 and 375.1.[2]

The stock market crash of October 24, 1929, and several days thereafter, signalled the beginning of a recession that was to turn into the worst depression in U.S. history. Unemployment rose from 7.8 percent of the working population in 1930, to 16.3 percent in 1931, 24.9 percent in 1932, and 25.1 percent in 1933. The boom that was built on the quicksand of easy money brought forth many years of want and suffering.[3]

From Ease to Super Ease

The money and credit policies pursued by the Reagan Federal Reserve are strikingly similar to those of the Coolidge Federal Reserve. Under President Coolidge, the Fed created credit to avoid depressions in 1924, and again in 1927. Under President Reagan, the Fed created bigger quantities of credit in 1982 and 1983 to facilitate economic recovery, and then created credit at rates never seen before to avert a threatening recession in 1985 and 1986. The Coolidge Fed planted the seeds for the Great Depression, the Reagan Fed is planting the seeds for a deep depression to come.

The Reagan Fed launched its credit expansion in 1982, when the 1981–1982 recession threatened to hold the whole world in its grip. The launch was designed, and actually managed to save, many bad debtors in the United States and abroad, from Mexico, to Brazil and Zaire, and thereby aborted the necessary corrections. Late in 1984, when more bad debtors faced difficulties, and the symptoms of maladjustment and recession appeared again, the Fed launched the biggest and longest binge of money and credit expansion ever. It conducted a policy of extraordinary ease until mid-1986, and then shifted to super ease, thereby generating an explosive growth of bank reserves and creating a huge speculation bubble. The reserves of depository institutions rose at an annual rate of 13.1 percent in the first quarter of 1986, 17.8 percent in the second quarter, 22.9 percent in the third and 21.5 percent in the fourth quarter. During this period, time deposits of commercial banks rose 1.9 percent, 11.8 percent, 25.5 percent and 38.5 percent respectively. The deposits of thrift institutions rose 3.1 percent, 20.9 percent, 23.6 percent and 23.7 percent respectively. The "narrowly defined" money supply (M1), consisting of coins, paper currency, plus all demand or checking deposits, rose 17.5 percent in 1986. It soared at a twenty-one percent pace since mid-April 1986, and literally exploded at a thirty-one percent annual rate since early November 1986. Money is created at record rates.[4]

The feverish pitch of the Fed money pump presumably serves two major objectives: to postpone the recession that is lurking around the corner, and to depress the dollar exchange rate to check the balance-of-payments deficits. Unfortunately, the binge is making matters worse on both counts, and is generating a speculative mania that inevitably must end in a spectacular crash and devastating depression. After all, the evils of recession cannot be averted by the very policy that breeds recessions. To prescribe more pumping action is like prescribing more alcohol to the alcoholic and more cocaine to the addict. It may temporarily alleviate the withdrawal pain, but makes matters worse in the end.

In economic terms, the money creation and credit expansion cause business distortions and maladjustments which recessions tend to correct. One binge following another may postpone the correction, but makes the maladjustment worse; it cannot avoid the depression in the end.

Rapid pumping action may depress the dollar exchange rate in foreign money markets, but cannot materially check imports, promote exports, and thus reduce the U.S. trade deficit. Surely, a decline in the dollar, versus other currencies, tends to make imports of foreign goods more expensive and American exports less expensive to foreigners. Yet, such changes in exchange rates are more than offset by the credit expansion and domestic spending spree. The trade deficit of the magnitude of $170 billion is caused by the credit expansion, and can be corrected only by credit stability and spending restraint.

The Fed money binge, which supplies commercial banks with all the money they want and the U.S. Treasury with all the money it needs to cover its budgetary deficits, is causing the quantity of money to surge as never before. It is producing the balance-of-payments deficits and fueling the two main events in the world's financial markets—the rapid decline of the U.S. dollar in the money markets of the world, and the stock market explosion in the United States. The decline of the dollar reflects a long-term trend, the stock market explosion constitutes an artificial bubble that is bound to burst.

The new euphoria on Wall Street, like all others before it, is driven by excess liquidity. In contrast, the American economy continues to linger in chronic weakness and threatens to sink into another recession. In January 1987, when the stock market exploded, leading economic indicators plunged one percent, which was the sharpest decline since 1984. New home sales tumbled 6.8 percent. New orders of manufactured goods fell four percent, which was the biggest one-month decline in seven years. Durable goods orders dropped 7.5 percent with military orders falling a record 9.9 percent. U.S. car sales in mid-February plunged twenty-six percent, casting a dark cloud on the future of the U.S. auto industry. Economic growth for the last quarter of 1986, as measured by GNP, was calculated at a 1.1 percent annual rate which, being less than the population growth rate, signalled further declines in American standards of living.[5]

While the U.S. dollar plunged to new lows and the economy lingered in stagnation, the financial structure weakened visibly. Seventeen banks failed in January 1987—nearly three times more than in January 1986. A growing vulnerability of the financial system, a chronic weakness of the economy, a weak currency, and a strong stock market—these are the ingredients for crashes and crises.

The Bubble

A sound stock market reflects the profitability of corporations. Representing an important part of the capital market, it reflects investors' anticipation of corporate earnings and savings. An unsound stock market loses touch with economic reality; it is driven by extraneous forces, such as central bank money manipulations and investor hysteria. The U.S. stock market today has lost touch with economic reality. While the profits of the Standard and Poor's 500 companies fell both in 1985 and in 1986, falling back to 1980–1981 recession levels, the stock index soared by some seventy-five percent. Their price-earnings ratio surged from 13.3 to 19 in just twelve months, which compares with just fourteen at the time of the 1929 crash.

Few voices in Washington favor monetary restraint and fiscal discipline. Even fewer suggest that the Federal Reserve cease and desist; no one is taking steps to balance the federal budget. The chronic weakness of the economy and the growing vulnerability of the banking system have locked the Reagan Administration into a posture of super monetary ease. It has become a runaway engine without an engineer with knowledge and courage to apply the brakes.

Runaway engines are fueled by high octane credit expansion and heavy debt leveraging. In the 1920s, a ten percent margin requirement provided the thrust that lifted stock prices to dizzying heights. The 1987 market is propelled by even greater leverage—corporate takeovers and buyouts that create billion-dollar mountains of "junk bonds," feverish speculation in stock-index futures that rest on margins of five percent or less, and index options that confer rights to these futures. To be bullish about stocks is to buy index futures or call options on stock indexes. When futures prices soar beyond the market values of the underlying shares, the spread then triggers massive stock "program buying" that lifts stock prices to the level of futures prices. Index trading accentuates the movements of the market, making bull markets more feverish and bear markets more depressed.

Bizarre Explanations

Soaring stock markets need expert reassurance that they rest on sound fundamentals, that the economic expansion has many months to go, and that the end is nowhere in sight. "Enjoy, enjoy," say the financial experts and investment advisors. Concocting fancy-built theories that seek to explain why the old explanations no longer apply, they reinforce the enthusiasm that carries the market.

Since 1982, the bull market has enjoyed support and endorsement by the *disinflation or deflation theory*, according to which monetary stability has created a long-term trend from real assets to financial assets. Disinflation is said to generate a long-term shift from real property, essentially land, buildings, precious metals, and many other real goods, to financial assets, such as stocks, bills, certificates, bonds, commercial paper, and other debt instruments. With disinflation in full force, soaring stock prices, so we are told, are merely catching up with other prices that soared in the past.[6]

The Federal Reserve actually practiced disengagement and "disinflation" in 1981 and 1982. Unfortunately, it returned to its old inflationary ways in August of 1982, and has pursued them ever since. Disinflation, in popular terminology, merely points up the fact that goods prices tend to decline during periods of readjustment and recession. In 1981 and 1982, some prices actually declined, such as those of basic commodities, capital goods, and real estate, but most prices continued to rise, although at lesser rates. Price inflation remained low, thereafter, because of a number of extenuating circumstances: the recession was world-wide, depressing goods prices throughout the world. Oil and other energy prices fell rapidly when OPEC disintegrated in 1985 and 1986.

Moreover, the Fed return to easy and then super easy money generated American buying sprees abroad and massive balance-of-payment deficits that saturated American markets with foreign products, keeping goods prices lower than they otherwise would have been. In other words, with the world on a U.S. dollar standard, foreign purchases of U.S. dollars through the sale of foreign products kept U.S. goods prices low and standards of living high. Of course, all such fortunate circumstances are bound to come to an end.

When the disinflation argument gave way to rising inflation rates, a new explanation was needed to explain and justify the bull market in stocks. The *foreign-cash theory* is serving this need in many quarters. Foreigners are pouring cash into U.S. stocks, we are told. With the U.S. dollar falling to new lows, versus other leading currencies, American stocks are cheaper today in Europe and Japan than they were when the Dow Jones averages were much lower. If the market were to pull back a little, U.S. stocks would be even more alluring to foreigners.[7]

Spurious notions and theories help to whip up the speculation mania, offering fanciful rationalizations to chronic losers. Surely, a falling dollar lowers U.S. stock prices to foreigners, which may entice newcomers to enter the market. Foreign investors with American stock holdings, however, suffer losses with every decline of the dollar. If both should decline—the U.S. dollar and the stock market—foreign investors would suffer from double jeopardy, which may lead them to shun U.S. markets. Keen foreign investors, just like keen American investors, are unlikely to buy more stock on the way down; they are likely to rush to the exits rather than add to their losses.

The foreign-cash argument, at times, gives way to a *signs-of-strength argument*, which is most popular with government officials and party politicians. The American economy is growing much stronger, we are told. Corporate profits are bound to rise and business conditions will improve. In the end, economic conditions will catch up with the stock market.[8]

Empty optimism is a kind of market stimulant—the digitalis of economic stagnation. Consumer spending is soft, the trade deficit is not improving, capital spending is sliding, and home-building has passed its peak; and yet, these optimists see lofty peaks ahead. The U.S. government continues to incur massive deficits that drain the capital markets. Congressional leaders want to raise taxes in the good old way: tax profitable business and productive individuals. They are proposing new levies on buyers and sellers of securities. They are suggesting delaying the scheduled cuts for upper income brackets under the tax reform passed last year. The reform had been made palatable to American taxpayers on grounds that they would get substantially lower rates while they would lose many deductions and exemptions. Having removed all the tax preferences, free-spending Congress now would like to keep the rates high; and yet, economic activity is supposed to catch up with soaring stock prices.

Yet another theory that seeks to explain and reinforce the market enthusiasm points to the *restructuring of corporate America.* It promises new profits through corporate takeovers and financial and managerial restructuring, through liquidation of unprofitable assets and excess capacity.[9] Unfortunately, corporate raids, buy-outs and liquidations are no substitutes for new investments and new production. They may boost earnings per share, but do little to raise labor productivity and increase output. They create mountains of new debt, especially "junk bond" debt that constitutes the weakest link in the economic structure. Yielding fifteen percent or more, junk bonds are unlikely to survive the coming recession. They are an open invitation to financial disaster for corporations, pension plans, and other investors seeking maximum yield on their portfolios. Savings & Loan Associations are holding more than $6 billion of junk bonds, which cast grave doubt on their financial future.

Many large banks are holding worthless claims against third-world countries that have no intention to repay. They are haunted by $100 billion of loans they have made to these countries during the ill-fated international lending binge of the 1970s. It cannot be surprising, therefore, that bank profitability has deteriorated, especially among the larger U.S. banks. Last year, nearly twenty percent of all banks insured by the Federal Deposit Insurance Corporation reported losses. Money-center banks, especially, are losing their good credit ratings. Just six years ago, eleven leading

U.S. banks had triple-A ratings; today only J. P. Morgan & Co. still does. Many bank customers have better ratings and can borrow money more cheaply than their bankers.[10]

While stock prices are soaring, the American banking industry is on a declining path. A heavy quilt of government regulations is smothering this vital industry. As long as government kept a lid on the interest rates they could pay depositors, banks were allowed to make money; however, that ended in 1981, when banks faced the competition with money market funds that are spared the high costs of being regulated. At the present, regulators and legislators are contemplating making matters worse. With Brazil's suspension of interest payments fresh in their minds, many want to force banks to grant concessions and resume lending to defaulting third-world countries, which would hurt bank earnings even more. Hurt and shackled, the American banking industry faces a fight for survival.

The situation is further aggravated by our extraordinarily low savings rate. Our political institutions overspend and overborrow while the share of after-tax income that is saved by the American people may be the lowest ever. It fell below two percent in late 1986; more than twice that amount was consumed by the federal deficits. The paucity of savings and their consumption by the federal government explains why a large portion of American plant and equipment is obsolete and uncompetitive in world markets. Much of the blame rests with the entitlement programs that guarantee generous incomes regardless of effort and thrift. Some blame also rests with the U.S. tax system that encourages debt through interest deductions and discourages saving by taxing it twice—once when income is earned and again when it earns interest and dividends.

In 1985, for the first time since World War I, the United States managed to join the ranks of debtor countries that owe more to the world than the world owes them, such as Brazil, Mexico, and Argentina. By late 1986, foreigners had invested more than $1 trillion in the United States, some $170 billion more than Americans had invested abroad. By the end of the decade, Americans may owe more than all third-world countries combined, which may raise doubts about American ability and willingness to repay.

Third-world indebtedness also presents a far more ominous picture than in 1929. Surely, a few South American countries failed to service their debt during the Great Depression; but most of it was productive debt that in time continued to earn a return. Present debt primarily represents consumptive debt, incurred by governments that squandered the funds on buying political power and self-aggrandizement. There are few new facilities of production earning an interest that could service the debt. Moreover, in 1929, most third-world countries were colonial adjuncts to European countries that guaranteed their debt. They all are independent now, badly mismanaged, politically fragmented, and deep in debt.

The international monetary order is more precarious by far today than it was in 1929. Then, gold was international money, incorruptible, unmanageable, and unchangeable. Today, the U.S. dollar serves as the international medium of exchange, managed by Washington politicians and Federal Reserve officials, manipulated from day to day, and serving political goals and ambitions. This difference alone sounds the alarm to all perceptive observers.

The stock market seems to be oblivious to the international situation. Its impressive ascent of more than twenty-five percent so far this year ignores all warning signals. It finds its justification in the belief that interest rates are relatively low, merger activity is robust, the economy is showing signs of strength, and foreigners are pouring cash into U.S. stocks. How long can wishful thinking continue to propel the market?

PART TWO

In Search of a Solution

7

PALLIATIVES AND PANACEAS

Dark clouds of economic and social disorder are gathering on the horizon. Most Americans refuse to see them, but are uneasily aware that a storm is coming. Although they had many opportunities to observe foreign storms from afar, they remain convinced that painful upheavals are alien phenomena that cannot happen here. To them, America continues to be just another name for economic opportunity and social justice.

Early signs of the coming disorder appeared during the 1960s, the decade of the Great Society, which launched a great number of expensive programs redistributing income and wealth. More signs came in sight during the 1970s, the decade of double-digit inflation, when federal deficits exceeded $364 billion and the U.S. dollar suffered repeated international payment crises. During the 1980s, finally, the decade of reckless borrowing and capital consumption, federal deficits often exceeded 5 percent of GNP, or nearly $1,000 annually for every man, woman and child. The federal debt doubled in just five years and soared by the trillions. While the federal government is indulging in massive overspending and overborrowing, the American financial structure is lingering in a precarious condition from which a painless recovery is rather unlikely.

A few courageous men and women are sounding the alarm. To the limit of their ability and strength, they are engaging in a bitter intellectual struggle with the forces of disorder. Addressing every important economic and social issue, they are writing books, essays, and articles and lecturing fervently on the furies of debt. They abhor the capital consumption by the now-generation and the burdens placed on future generations. In dismay and despair, they are pointing at the abyss toward which political society is rushing.

Some observers who should be able to see the coming storm unfortunately prefer to ignore it. They choose to remain popular with their fellow men who cannot and will not see the gathering clouds. They shun the world of intellectual combat and refuse to take a position on the burning issues of our time, on government debts and deficits, inflation, taxation, and unemployment. Fearful of unfavorable public reaction and personal repercussions, they huddle together and talk in soft voices while the storm is gathering strength.

Still other observers prefer to palliate the dangers and the evils. They embark upon lengthy analyses of the meteorological conditions of the disturbance and promptly arrive at simple solutions. They are rather popular with politicians and government officials because the solutions they offer are likely to be both empty palliatives and stale panaceas. They actively peddle their prescriptions for spending reductions, congregate at the seats of political power, freely mix with politicians and government officials, and patiently wait to be called to their councils. When called upon, they delight in idle argumentation about privatization and private enterprise.

1. PRIVATIZING FEDERAL FUNCTIONS
Seven Different Meanings

Most attempts at federal budget cutting prove to be rather ineffective. Powerful interest groups manage to impede nearly every effort to reduce the level of government expenditures, fighting valiantly to safeguard their entitlements and maintain or increase the spending. By contrast, taxpayers offer little opposition. Program costs are spread thinly among millions of taxpayers, amounting to a few dollars per capita. While the costs are dispersed, benefits are concentrated, which provides an important guidepost for politicians. It indicates that they have nothing to gain, but much to lose, from opposing particular spending programs.

Because of all the pro-spending incentives, few programs are ever reduced or terminated. Federal spending rises continuously and federal debt increases without an end in sight. Some observers despair about the democratic process, but many are convinced that there is a better tactic for spending control; there is "privatization." It assures continuation of the service, but transfers its rendition from government agencies to private producers. The efficiency gains that flow from competitive enterprise are to be used to cut spending.[1] Privatization is also said to pay rich political dividends. It creates powerful groups of constituents of providers and beneficiaries who profit from the program. They may be mobilized to give support to a privatization strategy and be used to build a powerful coalition for decisive spending cuts.[2]

At the present, we may search in vain for a coalition for spending reductions; but we do sense a powerful movement for privatization in all corners of politics, from the extreme right to the radical left. On the left, it may spring from the search for new government programs and the need for new sources of revenue. On the right, it may be a new version of the old vision of individual freedom and enterprise, or merely a natural reaction to more than ten thousand off-budget government enterprises that have sprung from local, state and federal governments in recent years. No matter what the motive powers may be, the movement should ring an immediate alarm with all friends of genuine privatization and put them on the alert about the actual meaning of privatization. If many reformers agree on an economic program, it is likely to be either empty and meaningless, or vague and fuzzy. In this case, the term "privatization" has at least seven different meanings and many more connotations that permit everyone to endorse it.

Upon cursory inspection, several versions become apparent immediately:

1. Federal assets may be sold at market prices to individuals who acquire unhampered ownership and control of the assets.
2. Federal assets may be sold at bargain prices to favored individuals.
3. Federal assets, such as AMTRAK, may be sold to individuals who remain under the jurisdiction of regulatory authorities.
4. No assets are sold, but private contractors are engaged to bolster expensive and unsatisfactory services of government enterprises, such as the Postal Service.
5. Private contractors are engaged to assist transfer and welfare

agencies, and make their programs more effective, from public housing to the administration of Medicaid and Medicare
benefits.

6. Privatization may take the form of a wide system of vouchers
    that give low-income people access to competitive markets,
    such as the education and housing markets.
7. Privatization may place loan assets in the hands of private
    investors, such as the portfolios of the Farmers Home Admin-
    istration and the Export-Import Bank.

All but the first of these versions of privatization are bound to
be disappointing in the end because they do not really reduce
federal expenditures; they merely seek to make the present system
more efficient. In fact, some are likely to cause government expenditures to increase as they call upon private contractors to
supplement government services, or create new classes of beneficiaries who hope to profit from government largess. Experience
also teaches that the new classes will not replace the old classes,
but instead can be expected to take their places in line with the
others.

Wherever these versions of privatization make the present system of transfer and entitlement more effective, they give it new
vigor and strength, and cause it to grow. Surely, a successful
voucher system that provides better housing not only is likely to
offer better homes and gardens for more people and cause the
housing industry to profit and expand, but also to boost the demand
for more housing vouchers and generate a demand for vouchers
for many other goods and services. Such privatization is likely
to extract more income and wealth from taxpayers, lead to more
deficit spending, and pave the way for more collectivization and
socialization.

Genuine Privatization

The only privatization that is worthy of its name is the sale of
government assets at market prices to individuals who acquire
clear and unhampered title to the property. Until the beginning
of this century, it was public policy to sell federal land to home-
steaders. Unfortunately, in recent decades, the policy has been
to take land from private owners and use it for "public purposes,"

such as irrigation or flood control, power projects, wilderness areas, or any number of programs. The federal government now owns more than thirty percent of all the land within the continental limits of the United States, and its holdings are increasing steadily. It now owns more than sixty-nine percent of the area of Arizona, seventy-one percent of Utah, eighty-five percent of Nevada, and ninety percent of Alaska.

It is rather difficult to assign present-day market value to federal real property, consisting of public domain property, donated property, and properties under the supervision of the Architect of the Capitol. This writer is willing to conclude that, at the height of the real estate boom in 1978–1979, when the federal debt was less than one trillion dollars, the market value of more than one million square miles of federal land probably exceeded the federal debt. Unfortunately, the debt has doubled since then, while real estate values have fallen substantially, which no longer permits us to draw this conclusion. It is fair to assume that a "privatization" of federal land not only could be made to cover the budget deficits and reduce the mountain of federal debt, but also substantially enlarge the real base of individual income and wealth.

Many other federal assets and enterprises could be liquidated and the proceeds be allocated to the reduction of the federal debt. In most cases, the sale would inflict significant losses on government, which usually manages to acquire assets in most inopportune moments and at exhorbitant prices. In 1979, when oil prices exceeded $35 a barrel, the federal government established the Strategic Petroleum Reserve (SPR). At the end of 1986, when the price stood at less than $15 a barrel, the level of crude oil in storage exceeded six hundred million barrels. Plans call for a 750 barrel stockpile that is to be maintained in a state of standby readiness, providing protection against supply disruptions.

Genuine privatization would liquidate the stockpile immediately because it makes matters worse. At the outset, its accumulation lent aid and comfort to OPEC, purchasing huge quantities of oil when OPEC was restricting world supplies and boosting prices. When OPEC finally succumbed to market pressures and oil prices retreated to recession levels, the SPR stockpile depressed prices even further. The stockpile, as well as current SPR policies, con-

tinue to disrupt the oil market, as did the federal controls over
U.S. oil production before 1981. SPR should be abolished immediately and its assets liquidated forthwith.

The Synthetic Fuels Corporation (SFC), another glaring folly
of federal politicians and officials, provides subsidies for "noncon-
ventional" fuel production. With world oil prices declining ever
since SFC creation in 1980, prospects for any commercialization
of synthetic fuels have diminished substantially. A program of
genuine privatization would terminate SFC operations and liquidate its assets immediately.

Sale to Favored Individuals

A form of privatization that has been practiced rather successfully by the Thatcher Administration in Great Britain is the sale
of assets to favored individuals. Government housing, for instance, is sold at bargain prices to low-income and public-assis-
tance tenants, who are likely to applaud the sale and oppose any
future attempts to renationalize. Similarly, government-owned enterprises are sold at bargain prices to their employees, who hope
to profit from the resale. To assure the highest possible market
prices for their shares, the new owners are likely to demand an
unrestricted freedom of sale to other individuals. Obviously, such
a policy of asset liquidation pays rich political dividends to the
resellers of the property, but it usually overlooks the fact that a
sale amounts to just another favor to a pressure group that reaps
benefits at public expense. The bargain price that is so attractive
to buyers is a distress price to taxpayers who provided the assets
in the first place. The fact that the sale may be the lesser evil
among several evil alternatives does not change the nature of the
taxpayer loss.

It is rather unlikely that this kind of privatization would find
much popular support if it were not for the bargains and favors.
At market prices, most government assets offered for sale probably
would be bought by investors and speculators who would want
to safeguard their investments and improve their yields through
cost reductions and productivity improvements. For the same
reason, public-housing tenants would strenuously oppose such
sales, just as civil servants would reject such a privatization of

their places of employment. In the final analysis, the sale to favored individuals promises to pay political dividends because it enriches some people at the expense of others, just like all other transfer and entitlement programs.

Many friends of the private property system nevertheless favor such privatization because it may reduce the economic scope of government and bring us a step closer to an unhampered market order. It may necessitate another hand-out in the short run, we are told, but will bear economic freedom in the long run. It may even turn civil servants and transfer beneficiaries into staunch defenders of the property order.

Surely, privatization as an interim step toward unhampered economic freedom deserves our undivided attention and assistance, but such an interim step must not be confused with just another step on the old road of transfer and entitlement. Privatization that safeguards old privileges, grants new favors to old interest groups, and imposes stipulations and conditions on the new owners is a make-believe privatization designed for gullible observers and investors.

Counterfeit Sales

Federal assets may be sold to individuals who remain under the jurisdiction and control of regulatory authorities. Such a privatization unfortunately does not change the employment of the asset in the process of production. Surely, the legal title to an asset does change from government to private hands, but its control, which is the economic essence of property, does not change at all; government continues to wield authority over the asset through one of its numerous agencies.

All sales of assets that have public-utility status are likely to be spurious and fictitious. The sale of the northeast corridor of AMTRAK to employees and other private interests, as suggested by the Heritage Foundation,[3] would merely transfer economic control from the Department of Transportation to the Interstate Commerce Commission and several other agencies that regulate the use of capital, and dispense immunities and privileges to labor unions. Sale of the two Washington airports, National and Dulles, to individual investors, which cost taxpayers some $2.3 billion to build and millions of dollars to support every year, would raise new cash for other federal programs, but would not in the least alter the economic status of the airports. Government agencies would continue to control every aspect of operation, would limit the maximum investment yield which stockholders would be permitted to earn, but refuse to give assurance of a minimum yield. Investors may do better by far buying Treasury bonds, notes or bills than to invest their savings in federal utilities offered for sale.

Private Contractors to the Rescue

The federal government is owning and operating some 125 economic enterprises, most of which are suffering substantial losses and serving their customers rather poorly. To reduce budget deficits and improve the service rendered, the enterprises should be privatized forthwith; that is, their assets should be sold at market prices, without regulatory restrictions, to anyone willing to operate them in competition with other businesses. Yet, this is not the intent of most privatizers. They would like government to retain ownership and control over the enterprise, but would be willing to have private contractors render some of its services. They would assign difficult and expensive tasks to private contractors, but retain profitable services and other activities that are likely to pay political dividends.

The Postal Reorganization Act of 1970 established the U.S. Postal Service as an independent federal enterprise. Annual appropriations to the Service now exceed $1.2 billion,[4] which include not only subsidies for carrying certain categories of mail at free or reduced rates, but also total actuarial costs of employee pensions. The hourly costs of work by some 740,000 Postal Services workers are estimated at $19.11, which are 33 percent higher than the hourly costs for equivalent work in competitive business. Moreover, USPS labor productivity lags far behind that of private couriers, which suggests the conclusion that every phase of the postal service can be contracted out at considerable savings to taxpayers. According to a Congressional Budget Office investigation, contracting out janitorial services alone would save $980 million annually.[5]

Such a conclusion is based on a simple assumption that must not be taken for granted in government enterprises. It assumes that the transfer of activity from government to private hands will reduce government outlays. Actually, the transfer may set civil service labor free, but is unlikely to terminate its employment and expenses. Government workers enjoy civil service protection, which bars dismissals no matter how much work is contracted out. Surely, it is unlikely that contracting the management of national parks to environmental and conservation organizations would bring any savings to the seven land-management agencies: the Bureau of Land Management, National Park Service, Army Corps of Engineers, Forest Service, Bureau of Reclamation, Fish and Wildlife Service, and the Tennessee Valley Authority. Contracting out undoubtedly would improve the service, but would necessitate additional expenditures. Similarly, replacement of the Legal Services Corporation with legal services provided through State Bar Associations and contracts with private legal clinics may not bring forth the dismissal of a single Legal Service Corporation attorney or any of his staff, but merely cause their transfer from one agency to another. In recent years, the mere attempt at agency reductions has led not only to frantic interagency shifting, but also to the creation of many thousands of off-budget government corporations that have greatly enlarged the scope of government activity. Surely, they all should be privatized; in reality, they are merely reorganized.

Private contractors may also be called upon to assist transfer and welfare agencies in their service to special beneficiaries, but it is rather unlikely that such assistance will help to reduce government expenditures. To contract out the management of public housing to tenants' organizations is unlikely to yield any savings. Instead, it is more likely to invite ugly tenant strikes and lead to expensive legal confrontations between the tenants' union and the public authority. Similarly, it is rather doubtful that a freeze of all VA hospital construction and a lease of hospital facilities from private owners would effect any savings. Instead, it would make available more private capital for VA use.

Voucher Systems

Many privatizers would introduce an extensive voucher system to slash the federal deficits. They would issue signed or stamped credit documents to beneficiaries who could spend them for designated purposes, under conditions stipulated, and in places clearly defined. They would establish systems of education vouchers, Medicaid vouchers, Medicare vouchers, health benefit vouchers for federal employees, subsidized housing vouchers, VA health care vouchers, and many others.

It is rather doubtful that the voucher system would provide any savings to the U.S. Treasury. On the contrary, a system granting educational benefits to certain beneficiaries may not only boost government outlays, but also greatly expand the sphere of government influence and control. It is unlikely to lead to a contraction of public education in any form, but undoubtedly would thoroughly affect private education. Private and parochial schools would have to meet the conditions and qualifications for earning the vouchers. After all, the authority that is issuing the vouchers and spending the money can be expected to state the conditions under which they can be used. In the end, any refusal to accede to such conditions may spell financial ruin to the resistor.

Similarly, a voucher system for housing would affect all sectors of public and private housing. The influence of government, which already is very extensive in this important industry, would reach ever further and touch every aspect of housing, as the voucher authorities would define the official conditions. Moreover, a voucher system would be likely to bring forth new governmental powers of enforcement over recalcitrant individuals who would refuse to honor and accept the official vouchers. Woe to the builder who would fail to meet the voucher conditions, and woe to the house owner or private school that would refuse to honor the voucher!

A health care voucher system for federal employees, veterans, or Medicare and Medicaid patients surely would not be permitted to diminish beneficiary services; nor could it be expected to reduce the present army of health care workers who render the services to federal employees, veterans, and Medicare and Medicaid beneficiaries. Surely, the voucher system would not be allowed to close a single veterans' hospital. Yet, it would soon permeate the whole industry—as do Medicare and Medicaid—with hospitals, doctors, and nurses scrambling to meet the voucher conditions. Indeed, it is difficult to find a trace of genuine privatization in the voucher system.

Sale of Loan Portfolios

Federal government loan asset sales have gained widespread support on Capitol Hill and on Wall Street. Federal politicians and officials are eager to turn the bulging federal loan portfolio into cash to meet Gramm-Rudman-Hollings deficit reduction targets. American bankers are eagerly awaiting the sales; when the Farmers Home Administration recently announced its intention to sell portions of its rural housing portfolio, thirty-nine unsolicited investment bankers applied to manage the sale. The Administration, too, is ready to promptly sell all new direct loans to private investors. In fiscal year 1986, the total amount is estimated to exceed $26 billion. In future years, it may be much larger.

Some privatizers would like the federal government to sell outstanding assets of the Guaranteed Student Loan Program to private collectors and investors. The impact of the sales, they tell us, would be not only immediate deficit-reducing revenue, but also the return of discipline and efficiency to the credit process. They heatedly argue with lawmakers and bankers about the details of the sales, especially federal guarantees and private insurance. Federal guarantees, they are convinced, would jeopardize the discipline and efficiency of the market place by reducing the incentive for the private investor to pursue collection, but undoubtedly would bring higher prices in the sale.

It is rather significant that these privatizers do not favor an immediate end of the programs on grounds of political economy and morality. On the contrary, they would like to render it more efficient. They do not question the role of government in credit affairs, nor the economic consequences of the proposed privatization. They merely engage in idle discussions about the efficiency of government in the collection business, and the sale of student loans to private companies better suited to the task. Unfortunately, they completely miss the crucial effect of the privatization program: it permits government to tap more private resources that heretofore escaped taxation and borrowing, to consume more private capital, and otherwise extend its influence beyond its previous bounds. This kind of privatization is completely counterproductive. If there were truth in politics, it would be called "the new collectivization-extension program."

At the end of 1986, the outstanding loan portfolio of the GSL program was estimated at $40 billion.[6] The portfolio carried over $2.2 billion in defaulted loans, with the present default rate at 11.7 percent and expected to rise to 13.6 percent by 1990. The sale of this portfolio, or any part thereof, would affect the loan market in precisely the same way a Treasury bond offering would; both would crowd out private borrowers. It does not matter whether the loans assets are guaranteed and insured, or merely left to the play of the market, they would all take the place of cash or other assets in the portfolios of private investors. The student loan may replace a mortgage loan, commercial loan, or just another government loan. In fact, it is even conceivable that such a privatization may permit government, in time, to pre-empt the entire loan market through massive credit activity and simultaneous portfolio sales. With off-budget accounting, it would not even show up in the budget, and the deficits would be limited to the defaulted loans not yet sold to private investors.

It is a sad commentary on the state of political and economic thought that conservative organizations and foundations that profess to promote the principles of a sound economy are using their meager resources to promote this kind of privatization. While the battle of the federal entitlement trough is raging and hundreds of billions of dollars of income and wealth are tossed about by the Washington agents of entitlement, the self-styled defenders of individual freedom and the private property order are proposing the privatization of the buoy maintenance program, the sale of National Airport, and the opening of rural postal delivery to private carriers. "Please support our national grassroot campaign," they urge their readers, "to help the President gather support for privatization."

Privatization is the new catchword that fires the imagination of many believers in political salvation. If they would only stop and listen, they would hear the persistent calling for more government and more spending.

2. A LINE-ITEM VETO
Continuing Resolutions

The annual battle over the federal budget provides an astounding spectacle that is both amusing and revealing. Despite countless committee meetings and lengthy hearings, the members of Congress fail to come to an agreement on revenues and expenditures. At the very close of the fiscal year, at midnight, September 30, the government is left without spending authority, causing its giant wheels to grind to a halt. Lo and behold, a few hours after midnight, in a dramatic session, Congress approves a stopgap spending bill enabling government operations to continue. There is no agreement on any one of the 13 appropriations bills required to fund government; but there is unanimous agreement that government must continue, benefit checks must go out, and Congressional pay checks must be issued. The members rise in support of a "continuing resolution" that authorizes the spending. Continuing resolutions thus take the place of the budget proper.

In 1986, Congress passed four separate stopgap resolutions to keep government from shutting down before it approved an omnibus resolution of $576 billion. The comprehensive spending legislation was necessary because none of the thirteen appropriations bills that were drafted to fund the federal departments and agencies had been enacted. Although it was the largest ever, the omnibus resolution did not include more than $400 billion for activities that are funded on a permanent basis, including Social Security, interest payments on the federal debt, and the bulk of Medicare spending.

The budget process is a free-for-all among the president and numerous special interest groups represented in Congress. Early in February, the president releases his budget for the coming fiscal year, calling for certain outlays and revenues. Early in March, the president's proposal is rejected for a number of reasons by the budget committees of both the House and the Senate. For all practical purposes, the rejection turns the budget process over to

Congress, whose members have difficulties reaching agreement on any of the appropriations bills. When no agreement can be reached, all proposals are combined into continuing resolutions, which in effect constitute the budget.

To the president and his administration, the budget process is most frustrating; it prevents the attainment or fulfillment of administrative goals and purposes. They are forced to watch helplessly how members of Congress openly thwart the president's efforts, blithely promoting their own political interests. The only retort at the disposal of the president is his power to veto the continuing resolution and thereby bring all government to a halt. No president has ever dared to resort to such drastic measures.

To deprive members of Congress of their partisan powers and "restore the balance of power," some critics of Congress would grant more power to the president. They advocate a "line-item veto," that is, the presidential power to veto spending for individual programs. Present budget procedures force the president to veto an entire appropriations bill containing hundreds of funding items, provided it passes both houses and reaches his desk, or veto the continuing resolution containing thousands of items, if he wants to block one particular program.

Several presidents have repeatedly requested the veto authority and included appeals for enactment in their State of the Union messages. Their followers in the Congress have introduced bills that would grant such powers. Some would provide a limited line-item veto authority that would permit the president to veto each of the thirteen appropriations bills when they are combined into one continuing resolution.

No Balance of Power

The presidential frustrations undoubtedly are matched by Congressional frustrations about the president seeking to prevent the attainment of Congressional goals and purposes. Both sets of frustrations spring from the fact that the sum total of goals and purposes exceed by far the available means, and from the circumstance that government in the United States is decentralized and its components frequently work at cross-purposes to each other. Federal fiscal activity may be frustrated in part by state and local government fiscal action, or vice versa, and presidential activity may be frustrated by Congressional action, or vice versa.

Decentralization of government engenders a number of difficult tasks, especially if government is to engage in redistribution functions and provide particular economic services. Political society not only must decide which goods and services government shall provide, but also must determine which level and branch of government shall provide them. The decisions may be influenced by several considerations, such as comparative economic efficiencies and political balance of power. In the United States, the desire for individual freedom also plays an important role in determining the division of governmental functions.

Before the dawn of massive government intervention in economic life more than half a century ago, the situation was much simpler. Federal revenue exceeded expenditures during most fiscal years, which created few occasions for fiscal conflict and frustration. Combined state-local fiscal activity generally exceeded federal government taxing and spending, which made the federal government a relatively unimportant component of government in general.

The Founding Fathers had planned it that way. There was fear in their minds regarding excessive power at the executive level of the federal government. Therefore, they gave the power of budgeting, as well as that of legislating, to Congress, although it was not well qualified to perform the budgetary function.[7] They granted the president some control over the budget through the right to veto, which the Congress may override by a vote of two-thirds of its members. In short, the Founding Fathers made the president execute the budget passed by Congress; they did not even call on him to help formulate the budget. They envisioned no "balance of power."

The president appeared on the scene of budget-making in 1921, when Congress passed the Budget and Accounting Act. It assigned the task of budget preparation to the president and created the Bureau of the Budget to assist him. Although the act has been amended a number of times, it continues to provide the basic budget procedure in effect today.

The budget-making process has been frustrating ever since.

The president is convinced that his election to high office by popular vote gives him a mandate for policy-making. Numerous pressure groups are calling for more government services and favors, which he is quick to promise, just like his fellow politicians running for office. As president, he is judged by his ability to make good on his promises and commitments, although he has no such executive powers. He is unable to deliver favors and benefits unless he manages to persuade the Congress to appropriate the necessary funds. His popular mandate may easily run up against Congressional refusal to finance his promises and commitments. Where he would want to increase expenditures, the Congress may allocate less, and where he would spend less, the Congress may appropriate more. Thus, Congress may tie the president's hands and force him to conduct policies he does not care to conduct. In his view, it is denying his mandate and usurping his power.

Conflict on Every Level

The tensions and frustrations in both branches of government are symptomatic of the general conflict that springs from the transfer and entitlement function of government. After all, government has no sources of revenue other than that which it forcibly exacts from its citizenry. Both the exaction and the distribution create economic, social, and political conflict not only between beneficiaries and victims, but also among the beneficiaries themselves, who are likely to argue about the mode of distribution, and among the victims themselves, contesting their assigned shares of the burden. The benefit and entitlement state is a conflict state on every level of its power structure.

In the noise of the entitlement battle, it is difficult to judge the priority of the claims. Both the presidential and the Congressional pressures for transfer funds spring from the same entitlement ideology that makes politicians and officials the arbiters of economic well-being. Both stand on shaky moral ground; both choose might over right.[8] Moreover, no matter how their claims are judged on moral grounds, they also need to be measured in terms of costs and consequences. In nearly every case, the president's commitments to exact and transfer income exceed by far the spending schemes of the members of Congress. Where individual Congressmen may engage in porkbarreling and logrolling, spending millions of dollars, the president usually spends many billions on "national needs" and "emergencies." His interests are nationwide; a Congressman's concern is likely to be special and parochial. The great spending programs of our time, costing hundreds of billions of dollars, from Social Security to Medicare and Medicaid, are the handiwork of presidents; the members of Congress fall in with the president and lend their votes to his ambitious undertaking.

While the president may be lobbying the Congress for new Medicare benefits, costing billions of dollars this year and every year thereafter, a member of Congress may hold out for a subsidy to a metropolitan transit system. The administration may want to phase it out, but members of Congress representing various districts receiving subsidies do not sanction the phaseout. They simply allocate the funds and mandate that they be spent. The Federal Aviation Administration may want to close an airport tower; Congressmen may mandate that it remain open. The administration may want to move an office, agency, or base; Congress may order that it not be moved. Congress may even require the federal government to build facilities where none are planned or wanted. To serve the interests of constituents, many members of Congress are voting their special interests without concern for the consequences of any individual program on the budget as a whole. Many are voting their interests without much concern for the objections of the president.

A Shift of Power

They are opponents of the line-item veto, arguing forcefully that the veto power would have very limited effects on federal spending, but dramatically shift power to the president. Many consider it "one of the most dangerous proposals ever made to the Congress." Some even call it a "dictatorial power."

Nearly one-half of government spending is not funded by appropriations bills. Entitlement programs, such as Social Security and other fixed obligations of the federal government, need no further Congressional approval and, therefore, would not be subject to a line-item veto. In contrast, defense expenditures, making up more than one-half of the money appropriated, would be subject to the veto. Without them, only 11–14 percent of the federal budget would be exposed to the veto power, and only a small fraction thereof would invite an actual veto. Careful analysis probably would reveal that one percent or less of federal spending would be vetoed if the president were given the veto power. It would not in the least alter the pattern of government spending, nor call a halt to Congressional porkbarreling and logrolling, nor alleviate the problem of deficit spending. It is a mere palliative, capable of drawing our attention from the real deficit dilemma.

Although the line-item veto may be no antidote to deficit spending, it surely would create more presidential power and alter the structure of government. It would be a powerful instrument of reward and punishment in the hands of the president. To reward members of Congress for going along on important presidential programs, the line-item veto would be held in abeyance. Loyal followers may even be encouraged to engage in porkbarrelling and logrolling and proceed assuredly without the risk of a line-item veto. The president's opponents, members of the opposition party, or lonely resisters to presidential programs, however, may face the line-item veto in all their special concerns and efforts. The veto power may single them out and hold their special projects hostage until they see the error of their ways and the wisdom of the president. In the hands of a president with dictatorial inclinations, it may truly be a powerful instrument, the use of which could be perfected to a fine art.

Congress may at any time override the line-item veto. In reality, the power is nonexistent, as long as the president manages to maintain a loyal entourage of at least one-third of the members of Congress. This should not be difficult with politicians whose votes are guided primarily by considerations of economic largesse.

To its ardent sponsors, the line-item veto is a potent remedy that promises to cure a great many evils. It may fairly and amicably divide the functions of the various branches of government, restore the balance of power, check the lust of spending, and hopefully balance the budget.

Unfortunately, there are no ready cure-alls for political ailments. The line-item veto power is no panacea. It cannot possibly calm

the political waters and break the habit of deficit spending. Nei
law nor regulation, Congress nor the president, can balance ,
budget if the people are enamored with the lore of political boun.
Reforms must prove unavailing if they are not accompanied by
reforms in political morality. They must originate with the people,
eager to do what they should do, and determined to do it because
it is right.

3.   A BALANCED BUDGET AMENDMENT
A Popular Movement

Some sponsors of the line-item veto would also amend the
U.S. Constitution to retrieve fiscal discipline. A Constitutional
amendment requiring a balanced budget, they assure us, would
restore fiscal responsibility and mark a new chapter in American
history.[9] The discipline of a balanced budget amendment is needed
to stop waste and squandering.

The movement calling for a balanced budget amendment came
to life in the early 1970s, when it became apparent that the budget
would never be balanced again. It has been floating about the
country ever since. It gave rise to a number of Congressional
bills which received Congressional attention in 1982 and again
in 1986. On August 4, 1982, a bill that requires a balanced budget
unless three-fifths of the members of both houses approve a deficit
was approved by the Senate by a vote of 69–31, two votes more
than the required two-thirds. A few weeks later, the House approved it by simple majority, but fell forty-six votes short of the
two-thirds majority necessary to approve a Constitutional amendment. When the Senate voted again on March 25, 1986, the bill
fell one vote short of passage.

Congress was pressed into action by a call of thirty-two states—
just two short of the number required for a Constitutional Convention to pass such a balanced budget amendment.[10] Since 1975,
state legislatures have passed resolutions demanding that Congress
convene a Constitutional Convention to consider a budget amendment. Since no such convention has ever been convened since
the Founding Fathers met to draft the Constitution, the thought
of a convention strikes fear in the hearts of most Washington
politicians. They are convinced that the convention would become

a "runaway convention" that would set its own political, social and economic agenda. To prevent such a divisive course of events, most members of Congress prefer to debate and adopt their own Constitutional amendment. They are likely to spring into action whenever another state is about to pass a resolution calling for a Constitutional Convention.

Hope or Hoax

The champions of a Constitutional amendment usually find fault with the U.S. Constitution. They point at a defect that grants special interest groups an organizational advantage over taxpayers. It permits such groups to lobby aggressively for government programs enriching themselves at the expense of all others, but diffuses program costs over millions of taxpayers. Benefit concentration and cost diffusion constitute a Constitutional defect that needs to be corrected.

The opponents to the balanced budget amendment usually point at the urgent economic problems of our time, such as poverty and hunger, unemployment, business and farm failures. Representatives of farm organizations lament about the farm problem; the spokesmen of older citizens' organizations dwell on the sufferings of the elderly, and the agents of labor unions voice their concern about depression and unemployment. Real economic problems, they assert, must take priority over balanced budget considerations. According to AFL-CIO President Lane Kirkland, the proposed amendment is designed to take public attention from the pressing issues of our time. It is "a hypocritical and cynical hoax."[11]

Defective Constitution

The advocates of the Constitutional amendment like to cite Thomas Jefferson who, just two years after the Constitution had been in effect, argued for a Constitutional amendment: "I wish it were possible to obtain a single amendment to our Constitution. I would be willing to depend on that alone for the reduction of the administration of our government to the genuine principles of its Constitution; I mean an article, taking from the federal government the power of borrowing."[12] To the advocates of a

Constitutional amendment, Jefferson's "single amendment" is the balanced budget amendment.

It is difficult to argue with the wisdom of Thomas Jefferson. In his great wisdom, he was fully aware of political temptations and follies, but he greatly overrated the ability of one generation to impart its wisdom to future generations, and for founding fathers forever to guide and direct the destiny of their descendents.

For nearly two hundred years, the U.S. Constitution revealed no particular defect that granted special interest groups an organizational advantage. Federal budgets were made to balance over a number of years, although wars and preparations for war brought heavy debt. Once peace was restored, the debt was quickly retired. The cornerstone of the present pyramid of debt that is measured by the trillions was laid only during the 1930s; it grew rapidly during World War II, increased by leaps and bounds during the 1940s and 1950s, accelerated during the 1960s and 1970s, and reached trillion dollar proportions during the 1980s. At the present rate of growth, it can be expected to double every few years.

To point at a Constitutional defect and suggest an amendment is to divert our attention from the true cause of the deficits, the great popularity of political spending. Politicians love to spend and the people love the spending programs. The diffusion of program costs does not explain the lack of opposition, nor does it reduce the costs and alleviate the heavy burden on producers. Most transfer schemes meet little opposition because the electorate loves the arrangement and partakes of the transfers. The result is chronic deficit spending at ever higher levels.

It is difficult to hold future generations to the strictures and limitations set by an earlier generation. Even if Thomas Jefferson's "single amendment" had been added to the Bill of Rights, it would be difficult to imagine Abraham Lincoln submitting to its discipline during the heat of the Civil War, or for the Wilson and Roosevelt administrations to abide by its limitation during two world wars. Similarly, it is hard to imagine that the present generation could be barred from acting in a way it wants to act. A Constitutional amendment standing in the way of a "greater society" through government spending would simply be ignored, repealed, or reinterpreted by a clever judge; or, government expenditures would quickly be hidden from the eyes of outside observers. No Constitutional amendment, no matter how comprehensive, could prevent the granting of benefits by government officials eager to bestow them to their beneficiaries anxious to receive them.

In purpose and design, a balanced budget amendment would resemble the Eighteenth Amendment, the Liquor Prohibition Amendment. It did not change human nature; instead it led to abuses and evils far greater than the amendment was supposed to correct. It was abolished by the Twenty-first Amendment, thirteen years later.

Raising Revenue

A Constitutional mandate to balance the budget could be interpreted to mandate higher taxes and more government intervention. Most politicians, including the amendment advocates, are likely to opt for boosting revenue rather than reducing expenditures. After all, they themselves launched the expenditures and created the entitlements; they would be rather reluctant to rescind them as long as they can raise revenues through new taxation. Many are convinced that business, especially corporations, enjoy excess funds that can be taxed away and made to balance the federal budget. Some would exact merely the "excess profits," that is, individual income they deem excessive; others would expropriate all capital income which they consider unearned and unjust. After all, if capital income actually is an unsavory exploitation gain that is withheld from working people, it should be seized forthwith and returned to the people. Yet, it is not very clear why "unearned" income should go to government for disposition by legislators and officials, rather than be returned to the individuals from whom it allegedly was taken.

Such a solution to the deficit problem unfortunately has many painful side-effects that make budget balancing rather unlikely. The lion's share of business profits consists of liquid capital that is used in production; only a small share of the profit total may serve the consumption demand by owners. In nearly all situations, to tax profits is to exact business capital, to diminish productive investments, reduce the number of jobs, lower labor income, and depress the levels of living. Surely, new tax levies may boost government revenue in the short run, but be insufficient to balance the budget. After all, the economic stagnation, which the new taxation may bring about, may not only necessitate more government outlays, but also substantially reduce government revenues.

Most Mainstream economists are reluctant to raise taxes as long as economic output is low and unemployment is high. In the footsteps of John Maynard Keynes, they prefer contracyclical government spending, together with easy money and credit, to stimulate economic activity. They are the original deficit spenders; they are not known to favor a Constitutional amendment to balance the budget.

A few naive friends of the market order may support the amendment in the hope that it may block further growth of entitlement spending, but they would be sadly disappointed if the amendment would merely open the gates to substantially higher taxation, followed by painful stagnation or even depression. As so often before, they are prone to cling desperately to the promises of politics when public attitudes and opinions disappoint them.

Other influential economists calling themselves "supply-siders" are convinced that deficits do not matter. They keep their eyes on the rates of taxation, convinced that taxes stifle production, lower labor productivity, and cause unemployment. They would lower income taxes to stimulate and invigorate economic output. It is most unlikely that they would cast their votes for higher taxes when faced with the mandate to balance the budget.[13] Yet, in politics, we must brace for the unexpected. After all, Congress has done the unexpected in similar situations. In 1932, in the depth of the deepest depression in U.S. history, it actually doubled the income tax and substantially boosted other taxes; it virtually guaranteed continuation of the depression for years to come. Under the strictures of a balanced budget amendment, Congress undoubtedly would boost taxes significantly, no matter how they would depress the economy. Just as in the 1930s, the American economy would sink into a deep depression, from which it would take many years to recover.

Raucous Opposition

The prospects for a Constitutional amendment in the foreseeable future are rather slim. The political opposition, which is both vocal and unrelenting, is blocking the way. It draws its strength from the armory of the welfare and transfer state, the very ideology that brings forth the deficits. In its judgment, the boon of benefits and entitlements exceeds by far the potential harm of debt and deficit spending. The amendment movement, which obviously does not share this appraisal, stands condemned for either greedily and covetously begrudging the benefits, or grossly overstating the effects of debts and deficits.

Surely, greed and covetousness are evil passions which nobody ever had the courage to own. They are sure marks of the absence of moral value and intellectual quality. Yet, it is rather surprising that these charges are levelled by the deficit spenders at the advocates of balanced budgets. If it is a fair assumption that the former represent the beneficiaries of the spending and the latter its victims, it permits us to conclude that the partakers are calling their victims "greedy" and "covetous" for objecting to the take. Obviously, there are no bigotries too gross for deficit spenders to create and adopt.

When they do not question the judgments and motives of pro-amendment individuals, the spenders are quick to point at poverty and hunger, depression and unemployment, and countless other undesirable conditions. Farmers lament low commodity prices and low farm income, the elderly moan about sickness and age, labor leaders wail about depression and unemployment. They are all convinced that government spending may provide a solution to their particular problems. Unfortunately, economic reality differs as much from their visions and convictions as it does from the hopes and beliefs of the champions for Constitutional amendment.

The economic well-being of all Americans, including that of farmers, workers, and the elderly, depends on American capacity to produce and compete in foreign markets. Economic productivity, in turn, is a function of productive capital and the investment of capital. When government deficits consume the lion's share of the capital coming to the market, economic progress must grind to a halt. Depleted and exhausted capital markets cause labor productivity to decline and unemployment to rise—especially in capital-intensive industries that are losing their ability to compete in world markets.

Most beneficiaries of government largesse, unfortunately, do not reflect upon the adverse consequences of capital consumption. They do not ponder over what they owe to others; their eyes are glued on what they can expect from them. They are always looking at the present; the future does not interest them. The golden age is now.

Backdoor Spending

A Constitutional amendment cannot impose temperance, prudence, and self-reliance on people who prefer self-indulgence, folly, and dependence. It cannot bring forth balanced budgets if the people prefer political largesse. If an amendment were to be imposed against their wishes, the people bent on deficit spending would find ever new ways of spending. They would easily circumvent the restraints of the amendment, just as they did during the Prohibition.

No Constitutional amendment calling for balanced budgets could close all potential channels of deficit spending. It is unlikely that it would block the present backdoors that permit Congress to engage in generous spending, not to mention future backdoors that can be constructed. At this very moment, Congress is shielding massive entitlement programs, expensive contract and credit activity, and popular off-budget operations.

Federal entitlements are rights, privileges, and benefits to which the beneficiaries—individuals or government agencies—are legally entitled. They range from massive programs, such as Social Security and Medicare, to relatively minor programs, such as compensation for pollution victims.[14] An entitlement binds the federal government to grant it and authorizes the judiciary to enforce it. It is unlikely that a Constitutional amendment would be allowed to prevail over it.

It is doubtful that a Constitutional amendment could be drafted to cover the numerous agencies that are federally owned and controlled, but deleted from the budget. The Export-Import Bank, the Postal Service Fund, the Rural Telephone Bank, the Rural Electrification and Telephone Revolving Fund, the Housing for the Elderly and Handicapped Fund, and several other government agencies are removed from the budget, but continue to carry out government programs.[15]

Although it is a part of the Treasury Department, the Federal Financing Bank operates outside the budget. Its lending is not counted as budget outlays; its total loans to federal agencies and private borrowers presently exceed $120 billion, which are off-budget. How would a Constitutional amendment be made to cover FFB activity?

The federal government controls a great number of privately owned enterprises that conduct government programs. There is the Federal Home Loan Bank System that promotes home owner-ship according to federal plan; the Federal Home Loan Mortgage Association that manipulates mortgage credit and mortgage mar-kets; the Student Loan Marketing Association, the Farm Credit System, and several other such organizations. They reportedly are holding some $438 billion in loan assets and can be expected, at the present rate of growth, to hold more than one trillion dollars in a few years.

In modern terminology, all this spending is "social progress"; to oppose it is to stand in the way of progress. Most Americans favor it, legislators enact it, and government agents administer it. A Constitutional amendment calling for balanced budgets, enacted under such conditions, may restore balance through sig-nificant tax boosts, but it may also lead to massive reorganization of government activity and spending. In particular, it may prompt a federal rush to the backdoors of government spending, and give rise to countless new off-budget agencies and private enterprises under government control. The possibilities of concealment, de-ception, pretext, sophistry, strategem, and plain trickery are end-less. Therefore, it is rather naive to believe that a balanced-budget amendment, enacted by the masters of subterfuge, could dampen the enthusiasm for federal largesse.

Deficit spending cannot be accurately told; the moral conse-quences are not visible to the naked eye. They require interpreta-tion and explanation. The economic consequences are highly deceptive, inasmuch as the spending is always visible while its costs are rather invisible—such as the investment not made, the service not rendered, and the economic good not produced. This is why, at least to dolts and dullards, government spending is always praise-worthy even while it lays waste to man's economy.

No political regulation, law, or amendment can impose integrity on people who prefer profuseness, dependence, and debt. They may have to learn from their own experience that debts and deficits are designed to serve the wishes of today and deny the needs of tomorrow. The American people may have to learn anew that a society that is living above its present circumstances is in great danger of soon living much beneath them.

8

TAXES AND TRIBUTES

Taxpayers and Tax Consumers

With the budget deficits in the hundreds of billions of dollars and the debt now counted by the trillions, many concerned Americans favor tax increases. They are represented by powerful leaders in the Congress and key tax-writing committees who consider it their first priority to raise taxes. The voices calling for tax increases are getting louder; some are calling for an immediate hike of twenty-five percent for many taxpayers.

Taxmen are encouraged by the fact that they succeeded in raising the levies many times before, without major repercussions to their political careers. The share of government extraction from personal income may stand near record levels, and yet, most lawmakers manage to be re-elected again and again. They appeal to the most vocal and most militantly organized pressure group: tax consumers, the most dependable American constituency.

Many tax consumers would simply raise the level of taxation to the level of expenditures; however, they are reminded by nearly all schools of economic thought that heavy taxation may lead to deep depression. To overlook the specter of economic depression that may follow new tax exactions is to ignore economic reality. Depressions invariably reduce federal revenues and enlarge the deficits, which may call for yet more tax exactions, in a vicious circle of ever rising taxation and deepening depression.

A compromise between taxpayers and tax consumers would raise some taxes and slash some expenditures until the budget is balanced. Yet, such a compromise merely intensifies the dilemma. It is likely to earn the wrath of taxpayers who are expected to bear the burden and of tax consumers who would lose their benefits.

The issue is further complicated by the confusion among economists, who can no longer agree on the very meaning and objective of taxation and expenditure, and on the significance of debt and deficits. Throughout most of American history, a tax was a compulsory payment to the government to defray the expenses it incurred in performing services for the common benefit. Fiscal policy was based on the assumption that receipts must equal government expenditures. During business recessions when revenues declined, taxes were increased or expenditures reduced. During economic booms when surpluses developed, tax rates were lowered or expenditures increased. No one seriously questioned the principle that budgets needed to be balanced.

Functional Finance

Over the past fifty years, Keynesian economics has brought radical changes to the financial affairs of government. It introduced "functional finance," the use of government finances for purposes other than the usual problems of balancing budgets. It made taxation an instrument of full employment and economic growth, and made fiscal policy an expedient of government control over economic activity. Federal revenues and expenditures no longer need to balance; they are supposed to reduce unemployment, stimulate growth, or check inflation. Surpluses are to restrain private spending during boom periods, deficits are to stimulate spending during recessions.

This mainstream view of fiscal matters helps to explain the massive federal deficits suffered in recent years. The deficits serve the "higher" objectives of full employment, price stability, and growth. This view also sheds light upon lawmakers who continually opt for more spending, rather than balancing the budget. As long as there is unemployment, price instability, or economic stagnation, they are likely to strive for the "higher" objectives. They deliberately unbalance the federal budget to balance the national economy.

The critics of functional finance raise two major objections:

1. The system is utterly inept for achieving the desired objectives. "Higher-objective policies" may actually bring about unemployment, stagnation, and inflation.

2. Functional finance bestows large powers on politicians and government officials, and grants them a command post over the economic lives of the people.

More than two hundred years ago, Adam Smith summarily rejected the very thought of functional finance: "It is the highest impertinence and presumption, therefore, in kings and ministers, to pretend to watch over the economy of private people. . . . They are themselves always, and without any exception, the greatest spendthrifts in the society. Let them look well after their own expense, and they may safely trust private people with theirs. If their own extravagance does not ruin the state, that of their subjects never will."[1]

Changing the System

The champions of functional finance at times may draw on the willing support by those lawmakers who would use the instrument of taxation to change the basic structure of the economy, in particular, to substitute a command system for the private-property, individual-enterprise system. In their hands, taxation is a favorite tool of government intervention. While, in the distant past, intervention through taxation was mostly limited to protective tariffs, restricting the supply of goods to benefit certain producers, contemporary objectives are more comprehensive. Some levies aim at influencing certain consumption, others are designed to affect certain sectors of production and trade. Still others are to change business customs and conduct. They all may gradually change the economic system.

Taxes may attack the substance of the private property order by destroying individual incentive and consuming business capital. Income taxes and business taxes may diminish the incentive to work. They may induce professional people whose services are urgently needed by society to work less and seek early retirement. They may induce young men not to enter business and become founders and promoters of productive enterprises, but to seek security and prestige in political offices and government appointments.

Confiscatory taxes that seize and consume what generations have built aim at the roots of the individual enterprise system.

Heavy death duties and highly progressive business and income taxes consume productive capital, and may cause economic stagnation and decline. Surely, such exactions do not destroy the real capital—factories and equipment—but they consume the liquid cash the heirs must raise to satisfy the tax exactions. In expectation of his demise, a successful businessman may sell out to his competitors to prepare his estate with readily marketable securities, such as U.S. Treasury bonds. The confiscatory death tax eliminates many family enterprises and promotes the growth of giant corporations.

To Equalize Incomes

Income taxation may aim at greater equalization of income and wealth through tax rate progression; however, this popular objective does not lead to a system that relieves the lowest income brackets from a proportional share of the tax burden. On the contrary, a number of able writers have shown convincingly that even the poorest people pay a higher percentage of their income in taxes than does the most numerous class of taxpayers. F. A. Hayek, eminent Austrian economist, found that it was not the poorest but the most numerous and therefore politically most powerful classes which were left off relatively lightly, while not only those above them but also those below them were burdened more heavily—approximately in proportion to their smaller political strength.[2]

Taxation is no simple fiscal matter. It presents problems of shifting, diffusion, and incidence, the difficulties of which challenge even the ablest economist. Every tax sets into operation a chain of reactions that affect industrial production, wages, income, employment, standards of living, mode of living, and so on. Most legislators probably are unaware of the numerous eonomic effects of the taxes they impose. They may be unaware that the steep graduation of the income tax accomplishes the very opposite of what it was meant to do. It perpetuates economic and social inequalities, and thereby creates a rigid class structure that divides society. The expropriation of high incomes effectively prevents formation of capital and wealth that facilitate individual advancement. How can an able newcomer from the wrong side of town rise to economic and social eminence if his "excess income" is expropriated at every turn of success? How can he challenge the business establishment with its hereditary wealth and position if he is prevented from accumulating the necessary capital?

On the other hand, old businesses can relax, turn inefficient and bureaucratic, because confiscatory taxation prevents newcomers from ever challenging the establishment. It is true, the tax progression prevents the rich from growing richer; but it also protects them from the threats of competition by ambitious and able newcomers. The rich tend to stay rich, and the poor are likely to remain poor, which gives birth to economic and social classes. Instead of individual effort and productivity, the coincidence of birth and inheritance becomes the main economic determinant in the lives of most individuals.

No matter how far-reaching the tax consequences may be, the level of taxation seems to have little or no effect on budgetary deficits. The Tax Equity and Fiscal Responsibility Act of 1982 imposed the largest tax increase in peacetime U.S. history. It raised federal taxes by $218 billion over 5 years. Although the leaders of Congress had promised to reduce federal spending by $3 for every $1 President Reagan would consent taxes to be raised, Congress increased spending by more than $1.25 for every dollar in tax increases. The deficits continued to grow.

In a brilliant analysis, Congressman Ron Paul concluded that tax increases may compound the deficit problems. "Taxes give the politicians more to spend—the additional revenues are never used to reduce deficits."[3] Throughout his distinguished political career, Congressman Paul favored tax reductions to bring spending under control and reduce the deficits. He was convinced that "only by shutting off the spigot of taxpayer money can the budget be brought under control and the deficit reduced. Just as oxygen feeds a fire, tax revenues feed the spending sprees of Congress."

The Gramm-Rudman Deficit Control Act

Many other legislators chose to attack the deficit problems by the most common route: they passed a law that outlawed deficits — the Gramm-Rudman Act. Many Americans hailed it as the turning point in the handling of the chronic budget deficit. With imperturbable faith in political action and the democratic process, they welcomed the Act as a declaration of sincere intent and the beginning of a new era in fiscal policy. Unable to agree on national spending reductions on a program-by-program basis, Congress finally agreed on an "automatic" approach that would eliminate deficit spending in 1991 by setting annual targets calling for deficit reductions of $36 billion during each of the next five fiscal years. If Congress fails to meet the target in any one year by agreeing on specific reductions, an automatic deficit reduction plan takes effect. The automatic process, known as sequestration, provides for equal cuts of both defense and domestic spending until the budget is balanced.[4]

A few observers remain unconvinced of the Congressional ability to solve the deficit problem. Even if the Act should reflect political honesty and sincerity, which are rare virtues in the world of politics, it lacks wide intellectual support and, above all, the moral foundation on which it can endure. Skeptics point at the undiminished quest for government programs and services which permeates political thought and policy. Every dollar of political spending benefits someone who has a vested self-interest in seeing his benefits perpetuated and expanded. Such interests are dominant throughout the political process, and their expectations and demands are met, time and time again. When the public wants gratuitous benefits, politicians cannot say "No." The collective demands upon the public treasury of all the special interests combined, therefore, tend to exceed the government's ability to pay.

The 1984 Act requires Congress to eliminate deficit spending by fiscal year 1991, some seven years and three Congressional elections later. Yet, every delay that postpones the correction of an evil aggravates the evil; it dulls the senses of the deficit spenders and magnifies the economic consequences of the deficits. The postponement of budget balancing also casts serious doubt on the sincerity of the Gramm-Rudman legislators. Many Congressmen who cast their vote for the bill do not expect to be in the Congress when the mandate falls due. The Act does not significantly limit their power to engage in politics as usual, but seeks to bind their successors. It should be obvious, however, that it is rather difficult for individuals in the present to induce individuals who come after them to live by their mandates. It is especially difficult for politicians who engage in freewheeling spending to bind their successors to unpopular spending cuts that may cost them their political careers. This is why every future Congress must be expected to reject the Gramm-Rudman mandate as an unwarranted imposition and interference with its own popular mandate. Even if the 1984 politicians who sponsored the Act should be back in Congress in 1991, few voters will remember the 1984 promises, fewer yet will hold them to their promises. After all, who believes the promises of an alcoholic or drug addict to go straight seven years hence?

The Gramm-Rudman Deficit Control Act is an excellent example of the art of politics. It permits federal legislators to vote for their favorite spending programs, and advocate and promise more, while the sequestration provision may negate their vote. Legislators may promise heaven on earth, but faceless sequestration prevents them from delivering it. Obviously, the Act will be the favorite target of political criticism until it is repealed, declared unconstitutional, or merely circumvented and evaded.

The sequestration plan provides for equal reductions in defense programs and domestic programs. If Congress should fail to agree on any cuts, then to achieve the $36 billion required deficit reduction, sequestration automatically cuts $18 billion from the defense budget and $18 billion from domestic spending. Both fields of government activity rank equal in the eyes of the legislators, which reveals a scale of values and priorities that is rather frightening. Defense expenditures, which are to protect the American people from the most ruthless tyranny ever known to man—Soviet communism—are placed on par with social transfers and entitlements that are to enrich some people at the expense of others. Protection of the nation from foreign aggression by nuclear weapons or conventional forces ranks equal with seventeen other functions and many more subfunctions, from general science, space, and technology to education, training, employment, and social services, from energy and agriculture to Social Security and Medicare. In short, political entitlement and personal re-election are as important as national protection from an evil system.

Moreover, if we bear in mind that federal expenditures on benefits and entitlements amount to nearly twice the defense expenditure, (some $600 billion vs. $300 billion), reductions that are equal in U.S. dollars cut twice as deeply in defense as in benefits and entitlements. A $30 billion reduction amounts to five percent of the latter and to ten percent of the former. After just five years of such "equal" cutting, we may speak of unilateral disarmament by the United States. It raises the disturbing question of whether disarmament actually is an objective of many legislators, or merely the by-product of an acute case of entitlement mentality. At any rate, a society that always chooses entitlement over defense is likely to lose both in the end.

It is significant that the budget deficit has actually risen since the passage of the Gramm-Rudman Deficit Control Act in 1984. It stood at $185.586 billion in 1984, rose to $221.629 billion in 1985, an estimated $215.984 billion in 1986, and may exceed $230 billion in 1987.[5] If there were truth in politics, the Gramm-Rudman Deficit Control Act would probably be called the Gramm-Rudman Deficit Obscurity Act.

Another Tax Reform Act

The 1986 Tax Reform Act confirms and complements the general trend. It is called "the most sweeping change of taxation in almost fifty years." Actually, the act is merely another effort at shifting tax burdens that work evil wherever they are placed. To broaden the tax base and eliminate many "tax expenditures" is merely another way of exacting heretofore untaxed individual income. It is true, the law lowers individual tax rates and reduces the number of tax brackets from fourteen in 1986 to five in 1987 and two in 1988. It reduces the top individual tax brackets from 50 percent in 1986, to 38.5 percent in 1987, and to 28 percent in 1988, but in order to retrieve the revenue lost, it increases the liabilities of corporations and top-bracket individuals by eliminating many tax preferences.

The new tax law repeals income averaging, which heretofore had permitted businessmen and professional people to save taxes in the higher income years through income averaging over a number of years. The law repeals the $100 dividend exclusion

($200 for married taxpayers filing jointly). It repeals the credit for political contributions, and the tax exemption of prizes and awards made in recognition of religious, charitable, scientific, educational, artistic, literary, or civic achievement. It repeals the itemized deduction for state and local taxes. Medical expenses of the taxpayer and of the taxpayer's spouse and dependents remain deductible, but only to the extent that the expenses exceed 7.5 percent of adjusted gross income.

The law disallows interest expense on consumer loans such as cars, boats, and credit card purchases. It repeals the capital gains deduction, and thus raises the tax on capital gains from twenty percent to a maximum rate of twenty-eight percent. As under current law, capital losses are allowed to the extent of capital gains, plus up to $3000 of ordinary income.

The new law severely limits losses from "tax shelters" that used to enjoy preferential treatment in the past, such as real estate, oil and gas, equipment, leasing, and research and development. It limits the losses from "passive activities" to the amount of income generated from similar activities. Passive activities are defined as trade or business activities in which the taxpayer does not materially participate, including all limited partnerships, interests, and most rental properties. The net effect of this repeal can be no other than a depression in the tax-sheltered industries, all of which are highly productive in meeting important needs, and the redirection of private funds toward tax-free state and municipal bonds, most of which are certificates of capital consumption and political waste.

The 1986 Tax Reform act is the fourth law in six years that ordered major changes in the tax structure. Many economic consequences of the act are uncertain, but we do know that there will be many future acts that will bring more changes seeking to shift an oppressive burden in the name of equity and justice. In the meantime, the Tax Reform Act imposes higher tax burdens on many businesses. It significantly affects manufacturers and capital-intensive industries that have relied heavily on investment tax credit and depreciation deductions to reduce their income taxes. In these industries, the decline is likely to accelerate, and unemployment to rise.

The Tax Reform Act of 1986, like any other reform act that does not honestly cut government spending and does not sincerely reduce the tax load on everyone, merely represents a temporary truce in the unending struggle over burdens and benefits. The struggle is primarily a bitter feud among various groups and classes of taxpayers with revenue-neutral politicians and government officials acting as referees, or with revenue-hungry politicians and government officials dividing and conquering alienated and disgruntled taxpayers. The 1986 truce is unlikely to last any longer than any other tax act before and any other that is bound to follow.

9

A LETTER TO THE PRESIDENT

A Noble Example

Man likes to mix illusion and hope, which may warp his judgment in council, but tends to quicken his energy in action. Men of letters like to wax eloquent about their world of thought, wander in hope, and cling to their illusions. They are quick to imagine that their letters are read and their counsels are heeded by men of action. Unfortunately, disappointment usually tracks the footsteps of their hopes.

When Governor Ronald Reagan was campaigning for the presidency in 1980, I had the opportunity to meet him at a conference in Honolulu, Hawaii. The Governor surprised me with astonishing knowledge of my essays and articles, expressing accord and compliment, even temptation to plagiarize them. According to the Governor, several of his weekly radio programs were based on my essays and articles. It cannot be surprising, therefore, that on the occasion of his inauguration as President of the United States, I felt free to proffer my advice.

January 12, 1981

President Ronald Reagan
The White House
Washington, D.C.

Dear Mr. President:

It can be done! The federal budget can be balanced and the U.S. dollar be saved.

It can be done promptly and least painfully with the following spending cuts:

1. To set a stunning example of leadership and to illuminate the fiscal emergency, the President himself should take a salary cut of 50 percent.

2. The legislators who are the guardians of the public purse should be called upon to take a cut of 25 percent. Such an appeal would confront and confound their spending predilection.

3. All federal transfer spending, i.e. expenditures that benefit someone at the expense of someone else, should be frozen for a period of one year, which would save more than $40 billion.

4. This modest reduction in federal spending would bring immediate relief to our exhausted capital markets, which in turn would reduce interest rates and the carrying charges of the federal debt. A mere drop of 3 percent would decrease the federal interest charges on more than $900 billion by more than $27 billion. Altogether, these savings would suffice to restore fiscal integrity. They would give new life to the U.S. dollar and bring new hope to the people.

It can be done with courage and dedication.

Sincerely,

Hans Sennholz

Advice is seldom welcome. Those who need it most like it least. The letter, which was placed in the hands of the president by a well-known U.S. senator, remained unanswered; the advice was ignored. It tried to make two simple points of counsel:

1. there is transcendent power in example—we lead others when we walk upright;

2. transfer income differs from production income—it is derived from and limited by the latter.

The example set by eminent men on the public stage of the world is more influential by far than any rule or regulation. The example set by the President of the United States is probably the most important object lesson of all, with the eyes of the world upon him, the leader of the leading nation of the world. Mr. Reagan, unfortunately, did not choose to rule by example. Instead, he limited himself to enumerating some principles and precepts of the individual enterprise order. He eloquently articulated the cause of freedom, but utterly failed in its implementation. He was a spokesman, not an organizer; a salesman, not a chief executive who leads by example. He waxed eloquent about the virtue of frugality and integrity, but rendered the noisiest and most expensive pressure groups untouchable and approved generous raises to the army of legislators and civil servants. No real attempt was made to use the Executive Office as an example and vehicle to promote fiscal integrity.

President Reagan did not choose to set a noble example by taking a salary cut, nor did he call upon the U.S. Congress to suffer a reduction. Instead, during his Presidency, Congressional pay was boosted more often than under any other president, nearly every year, in 1983, 1984, 1985, 1986, and 1987. His own remuneration, together with the perquisites of the Presidency, soared to more than $50 million a year.[1]

A Splendiferous Stage

No individual on the face of the earth enjoys a life style more illustrious, grandiose, and expensive than the president of the United States. No monarch, emperor, or potentate in the history of the world ever ruled in a setting as splendid, elaborate, and luxurious as the president of the United States. No capitalist or entrepreneur, no matter how wealthy and exotic he may be, can compare his level of living with that of the president. Surely, his annual salary is only $200,000, taxable. He is entitled to $100,000 travel allowance and $12,000 entertainment allowance, both tax exempt. The largest part of his compensation by far consists of fringe benefits and perks. He and his family reside rent free at the White House; a fleet of automobiles with a detachment of chauffeurs is at his disposal; some twenty-five Secret Service men, paid by the Treasury Department, guard him. A yacht, belonging to the Navy, operated by the Navy, and maintained by Navy appropriations, is waiting at a Potomac pier. A fleet of presidential airplanes and helicopters owned and operated by the Air Force is waiting at nearby airports. A stable of horses for riding is supplied by the Army. A private Pullman car with armor-plated bulletproof windows is at his disposal. A personal physician supplied by the armed forces attends to his and his family's physical needs; all Army and Navy hospitals stand ready to serve him. More than one hundred policemen are assigned to guard the White House and its grounds and a large staff of domestic servants are waiting on him day and night.

When the president leaves office, his pension amounts to $69,630 a year. He has free mailing privileges, free office space, and draws $96,000 a year for office help. He receives $150,000 for staff assistance during the first thirty months after his term of office has ended. During the first six months of retirement, the president and the vice-president also share $1 million for administrative help in winding up the affairs of their offices.[2]

During his terms of office, when nearly two trillion dollars were added to the federal debt, President Reagan did not see fit to suffer any reduction in his presidential fringes and perks, nor did he call on the Congress to set an example of fiscal frugality. The splendor of the presidential court and the congressional offices remained undiminished; in fact, they contributed their share to the budgetary deficits. The president's fringe benefits and perks now amount to many millions of dollars; his salary constitutes a small fraction of his total compensation.

Presidential Salaries

1789–1873	$ 25,000		
1873–1906	50,000		
1906–1909	50,000	+ $	25,000 travel expenses
1909–1948	75,000	+	25,000 travel expenses
1948–1949	75,000	+	40,000 travel expenses
1949–1969	100,000	+	50,000 travel expenses
1969–present	200,000	+	100,000 travel expenses
		+	12,000 entertainment

Source: Joseph Nathan Kane, *Facts About the Presidents, ibid*, p. 417.

Until 1857, the presidents paid their secretaries from their private funds. A law of 1857 authorized them to employ one private secretary. In 1900, they were authorized to employ one secretary and two assistants; in 1948, the number was raised to one secretary with six administrative assistants. In fiscal year 1987, the budget calls for White House Office Funds of $25.059 million. Total expenses of the Executive Office of the president are given at $114.606 million.[3]

From $6 a Day to $89,500 a Year

Without presidential leadership, the U.S. Congress disclaimed all responsibility for budgetary deficits and, spending lavishly on favorite transfer causes, ascribed the growing deficits to the president's refusal to provide the necessary funds through higher taxes. Listening rarely, but always speaking, most members of Congress are working diligently to sustain or expand government; they have no intention whatever to carry out the cut-and-trim policy the president is articulating. Having led their favorite constituents to the federal waterholes and having dispensed trillions of dollars of benefits, they themselves like to line up occasionally for a generous take in benefit and salary increases. They may even blatantly circumvent the will of the people by avoiding public debate on the pay raise package, allowing pay raises for themselves and other top government officials to take effect without a recorded vote. Making matters worse, a pay grab may follow a cost-of-living increase, which Congress quietly slips itself in the omnibus resolution. In short, the lawmakers who incur one hundred billion dollars of debt every year callously and cowardly may give themselves two pay raises in the space of a few months. Their take is a clear interpreter of their thought and philosophy of government.

It is vain to expect any advantage from politics if politicians are not sincerely just and honest in their actions. It is vain to expect frugality and economy of politicians who themselves cannot make ends meet. They may wax eloquent about the need for government to compete successfully with the private sector for the most talented men and women willing to enter politics, and then slip themselves another raise. They may use the resentment and envy of the poor against the rich by posturing as poor politicians representing the poor, and depicting the denial of a salary increase as surrender of government to the rich. Government must not become a prerogative of the rich, they pontificate; therefore, we deserve another raise.

The actions of men are the best interpreters of their thoughts. The Founding Fathers created the Constitution that reveals their thought on the question of Congressional compensation. Article 1, Section 6, stipulates that "Senators and Representatives shall receive a compensation for their Services, to be ascertained by Law, and paid out of the Treasury of the United States." The Constitution left the delicate question of what that compensation shall be to Congress itself. The inevitable result was to make Congressional pay a political issue that has plagued Congress throughout its history.

At various times, the American public strongly opposed Congressional pay increases, which led to numerous election defeats of members voting themselves increases. At other times, Congressional pay was permitted to rise without much opposition. No matter what the public attitude may have been throughout 200 years of Congressional history, a mere glance at the members' compensation seems to reveal an astonishing correlation of pay and policy. When the Founding Fathers, many of whom were men of genius, were meeting in the early Congresses, their remuneration was $6 per diem. They balanced the budget every year and promptly repaid the heavy debt incurred during the War of Independence. Two hundred years later, their successors regularly incur budget deficits, amass a national debt measured in the trillions, disclaim all intention to repay the debt, and slip themselves two increases within four months, without even openly voting for them. They now draw $89,500 per year, supplemented by generous fringe benefits, such as free mailing privileges, free office space in a federal building in their home state or district, an expense account for travel, free telephone and telegraph, stationery, office expenses and equipment, free publications, radio and television recording studios at minimal rates, bargains at Capitol Hill shops, dining rooms, barber and beauty shops, luxurious swimming pools, saunas with masseurs and masseuses, gymnasiums, health protection benefits, life insurance and generous pensions, free legal counsel, etc., etc.

In the early days of the Republic, senators and representatives had no staff and no expense accounts. Today, 535 members of Congress employ a staff of more than 18,000 civil servants. The

Tax Foundation estimated in 1982 that each senator costs taxpayers $2.3 million in direct outlays a year, and representatives $836,000. If the costs of office space in the grandiose temples of government were to be added, the costs of each member of Congress would be many millions of dollars. The Solons of the entitlement society obviously do not walk in the footsteps of the Founding Fathers. The merit of great men is not understood by those who lack merit; greatness speaks only to greatness.

Congressional Salaries

Year	Salary		Year	Salary	
1789–1795	$ 6	per diem	1935–1947	$10,000	
1795–1796	6	(House)	1947–1955	12,500	
	7	(Senate)	1955–1965	22,500	
1796–1815	6	per diem	1965–1969	30,000	
1815–1817	1,500	per year	1969–1975	42,500	
1817–1855	8	per diem	1975–1977	44,600	
1855–1865	3,000	per year	1977–1980	57,500	
1865–1871	5,000		1980–1982	60,662	
1871–1873	7,500		1983	60,662	(Senate)
1873–1907	5,000			69,800	(House)
1907–1925	7,500		1984	72,600	
1925–1932	10,000		1985	75,100	
1932–1933	9,000		1986	77,400	
1933–1935	8,500		1987	89,500	

Source: Congressional Quarterly's *Guide to Congress*, Washington, DC, 1982, p. 572; Congressional Quarterly, *Almanac*, 97th Congress, 1982, p. 544.

10

THE COMING STORM

Deep in Debt, in Grave Danger

Great changes are bound to come to us. The federal debt, which is counted by the trillions of dollars, may be an inconvenience now, but is likely to become a calamity tomorrow. It may dissipate our levels of living, foster inflation, and cause millions of Americans to sink into poverty and despair. The debt habit is the brother of poverty.

The U.S. government has run deficits during 24 of the last 25 years. In the past ten years, the deficits have averaged 2.5 percent of GNP. Last year, the deficit was over five percent, amounting to nearly $1,000 for every man, woman, and child in the United States. To cover the deficits by increasing taxes would mean an extra tax of $2,400 on each American household.[1] If business were to bear the load, it probably would sink into deep depression, from which it would take many years to recover.

The magnitude of federal indebtedness is awesome. It has more than doubled during the last five years, and now exceeds $2 trillion, or $10,000 per person. If we were to add contingency liabilities and obligations, we would arrive at federal obligations in excess of $13 trillion, or more than $65,000 for every man, woman, and child. Other debt, corporate and personal, now exceeds more than $7 trillion, or $35,000 per person. Debt on all levels comes to more than treble the nation's output of goods and services.[2]

The federal debt is a predicament for which there is no easy solution. Our political apparatus of transfer and entitlement has lived, and continues to live, far beyond our means; it overborrows and overconsumes, wearing away and depleting the very apparatus of production. To bolster our sagging living standards, we have become the largest debtor country in the world and, in a few years, may be deeper in debt than all developing countries combined.

Since there is no orderly way to liquidate the federal debt, we must brace for a payment crisis. One way or another, the era of federal deficits and debts will draw to a close, the awesome burden of federal debt will be erased, bringing in its wake extensive economic dislocation, depression, and unemployment. Wage rates will plummet as labor productivity falls, and capital income will plunge as financial assets are written down or written off.

End of an Era

Any one of several events may trigger the coming crisis that will signal an end to the debt and deficit era and the beginning of the payment era. Six such situations readily come to mind:

1. Foreign investors may be frightened by American conditions and, therefore, withdraw the bulk of their funds, causing a severe squeeze in U.S. credit markets; or, they may withdraw some funds in reaction to credit strains in foreign financial markets. When the markets in Tokyo, Hong Kong, Singapore, or London face a credit squeeze, the New York market may suffer a run. As a debtor country, the United States is highly vulnerable to withdrawals of foreign investments.

    During the early and mid-1980s, foreign investments enabled the federal government to finance its huge deficits rather painlessly. Foreigners invested their savings in Treasury obligations and U.S. corporate issues, which permitted Americans to consume not only their own incomes, but also foreign savings. Without this foreign help, the strain on American credit markets would have been far greater, interest rates would have been higher, and the federal government would have crowded out more business activity. Without foreign help, the Federal Reserve System would have to purchase more Treasury obligations, which would have created more U.S. dollars and raised goods prices. When, for any reason, foreign investments come to a halt, or even are liquidated and withdrawn, all these financial effects are bound to appear.

2. The world's financial order is unsustainable in its present form; at any moment, it may suffer a massive credit collapse. Throughout the 1970s, many big city banks lent so much money so unwisely to third world countries, many of which lack both ability and intention to repay the loans. Latin America alone carries a foreign debt of more than $360 billion, most of which was pressed on them by eager U.S. bankers seeking to recycle OPEC deposits. Black African countries chafe under a debt of more than $50 billion. Most of these debtors favor immediate repudiation of their debt unless the loans are promptly "rescheduled" and the International Monetary Fund and the Federal Reserve System keep pumping new money into their treasuries.

Foreign debt tends to become onerous when more than twenty percent of a country's export earnings are needed to service medium and long-term debt. According to a 1984 Morgan Guarantee Trust Company survey, forty of eighty-one countries need more than twenty percent. Zaire, Argentina, Mexico, Chile, Brazil, and Morocco use approximately fifty percent. With short-term debt included, the rates exceed 100 percent in some countries; they stand at 150 percent in the Philippines, Uruguay, Israel, and Mexico, and at 200 percent in Argentina.[3]

In many third world countries, the populace lacks the business ethics that are basic to debt repayment. Repayment, under duress and at the request of the IMF, is viewed as a painful austerity measure which capitalist bankers like to impose on poor countries. It may lead to economic, social, and political flare-ups and the overthrow of governments. Suspensions of payment, moratoria, and "reschedules," on the other hand, may enhance the popularity and political position of the defaulter.

Without federal government help, the American banking system could not withstand the shock of third world loan default. The large money-center banks would suffer staggering losses that would exceed their capital and surplus. According to Data Resources, Argentina, Brazil, Mexico, and Venezuela alone owe Citibank 135 percent of equity, Bank of America 158 percent, Chase Manhattan Bank 162 percent, Manufacturers Hanover 193 percent, Morgan Guaranty 139 percent, Chemical Bank 141 percent, Bankers Trust 162 percent, and First Chicago 128 percent.[4] The third world debt is clearly unpayable, and many bankers are rather unprepared for the inevitable default.

Many Savings and Loan Associations are sharing the fate of the big city banks. Surely, they cannot be charged with making too many poor loans; they faithfully lived by the strictures of legislation and regulation, financing the construction and purchase of homes through mortgage loans. They, nevertheless, are in dire straits because inflation, together with regulation, has squeezed them dry. Legislation narrowly circumscribed the rates of interest they were permitted to pay their passbook depositors, and inflation raised the market rates of interest far above those imposed on the thrifts, which lifted them right out of the competition for funds. They lost many billions in deposits, which sought higher interest rates in money-market funds and other instruments. To survive the painful drain of savings and safeguard their liquidity, the thrifts then had to "purchase" funds through the sale of certificates at interest rates far above those earned on old mortgage loans. Many suffered, and continue to suffer, staggering losses which are casting doubt on their survival.

With many thrifts at death's door, legislation and regulation granted them the freedom to offer commercial banking services and compete with all other banks. Unfortunately, this new freedom may have come too late; the losses suffered in the past are irretrievable. Although interest rates have come down in recent months, the passbook rate continues to discourage deposits, and encourages withdrawals.

The end of many Savings and Loan Associations is coming in sight. The reinflation of the U.S. dollar, bolstering the international financial order, and rescuing bankrupt debtor countries and foolish city bankers will, in time, rekindle the fires of inflation and cause interest rates to resume their upward march. Many thrifts will probably survive through mergers with other financial institutions, which will further weaken the financial structure of the buying institutions. Others will wait to be rescued by the authorities.

3. A deep recession may shake the financial structure in its foundation and signal the end of the deficit era. If the federal budget deficit amounts to $200 to 250 billion in years of economic prosperity and growth, as it does today, what will it be in the coming recession? Surely, a recession is coming with the inevitability of economic law and the manipulation of money and credit by Federal Reserve officials. The recipe of contracyclical spending and credit expansion is as popular today, in political circles, as it ever has been since the 1930s. This is why we expect annual budget deficits of $300 billion to $500 billion in the coming recession, which may further weaken the financial structure and push it to the breaking point.

The lion's share of budget deficits of such magnitudes will need to be monetized, that is, used to increase the stock of currency and credit. The Federal Reserve system will purchase massive quantities of Treasury obligations, thus releasing new Federal Reserve money to the public. As private economic activity contracts, government expands and consumes a larger share of economic resources. In time, goods prices will soar, and interest rates will rise, inflicting new losses on stock and bond investors.

It is unlikely that foreign investors will again come to our rescue. They may be frightened not only by the magnitude of federal deficits, but also by the economic ideology and policy that breed these deficits. A society capable of living persistently beyond its means may have lost the integrity and willpower to repay its debt. After all, repayment of debt requires living below one's means, to which a deficit society does not readily submit.

Foreign investors, just like domestic investors, are unlikely to invest their savings in American equities and obligations when they are suffering losses. In a recession, stock and bond prices are likely to fall, which may persuade foreign investors to recall their funds while they can. In short, when the federal government indulges in recession spending, and incurs deficits counted in hundreds of billions of dollars, while foreign investors are withdrawing some of their trillion-dollar holdings, the American financial structure may come under pressure and the deficit era may draw to an end.

4. The rising burden of interest on the growing debt may, in time, become so irksome to the deficit generation that it may want to "reform" the debt structure. The federal government now spends 41¢ of every dollar on direct benefit payments for individuals, 28¢ on national defense, 10¢ on grants to states and localities, 6¢ on other federal operations, and 15¢ on net interest on its debt.[5] Interest outlays are directly affected by the size of the debt and the going rate of interest. If interest rates should double again, which can be expected if the rate of inflation should double and triple again, the federal government may have to allocate 30¢ or more of its expenditure dollar to service its debt. Transfer benefits may have to be curtailed so that bondholders can be paid, which does not endear bond holders and the interest they earn to transfer beneficiaries. If the size of the federal debt should double again, as it did during the first five years of the Reagan Administration, interest charges also may double. At some point, the transfer generation may feel deprived and oppressed; it may press for a "reform" that reduces the interest burden to allocate more funds for direct benefit payments.

A growing burden of debt and interest may frighten investors. Surely, a rising rate of interest may provide a premium for bearing the growing risk of loss and depreciation. Yet investors may be fearful that the higher rates of return may not warrant the growing risk of default. They may seek refuge in real goods, or escape to the underground economy where they hope to survive the coming storm. Foreign investors may be first to depart.

5. The growing specter of protectionism here and abroad may signal an end to the deficit era and a beginning of the inevitable adjustment. With growing trade deficits resulting from the dollar inflation and the capital consumption, the United

States is turning increasingly protectionistic. When, during much of the 1940s through the 1970s, the trade balance was in surplus, the U.S. government championed freedom of international trade; when, during the 1980s, the situation deteriorated drastically, it turned protectionistic. Industries from textiles to motorcycles, automobiles, and steel lobbied to exclude foreign products from their markets, and the Reagan Administration readily granted protection through a variety of protectionistic measures. It is significant that the opposition party, which throughout its history has spearheaded the cause of international trade, seems to have become even more sympathetic to protectionism than the party in power.

In a world dependent on international trade and commerce, and staggering under a heavy load of international debt, no policy is more destructive than protectionism. It cuts off markets, eliminates trade, causes unemployment in the export industries all over the world, depresses the prices of export commodities, especially farm products of the United States. It is the crowning folly of government intervention. Protectionism in the form of another Hawley-Smoot Tariff Act of June, 1930, which turned a recession into the Great Depression, or in any other guise, would play instant havoc with financial markets and signal the beginning of another depression. In a poignant way, a depression calls a halt to an era of debts and deficits.

6. Economic life is encompassed by political conditions and social institutions. When they are conducive to economic productivity and output, economic conditions may improve and bring forth general prosperity. When they turn increasingly hostile to economic effort, conditions are bound to deteriorate. This is why investors and entrepreneurs must always keep an eye on the body politic.

The American political stage has many actors who would call a halt to the deficit era. It is unlikely that they would reduce federal outlays, except on national defense; instead, they may significantly boost taxes, especially business taxes, to cover the deficits. Some may rely more heavily on the money creating powers of the Federal Reserve System and its legal tender powers. Others may return to ancient solutions—government regimentation and regulation. As the absolute monarchs of the sixteenth through eighteenth centuries ruled over their subjects' financial affairs, so may the financial authorities of the 1990s rule us. The coming elections will shed more light on the economic outlook for the 1990s.

Man is blind to the future. Yet he is always looking to the future; the present does not satisfy him. His hopes and dreams, whatever they may be, lie further on. Some individuals are convinced that all will be well with the world, and that all debt will be paid in the end. Others are inclined to analyze the facts and realities. With all their knowledge and wisdom, they can see no possible way of painless extrication from the debt predicament. Yet, they believe that the era of deficits and debts is bound to draw to a close, and that the awesome burden of debt will soon be reduced by rampant inflation, acute deflation, strict regulation, or a combination thereof.

Rampant Inflation

To many economists, the most likely resolution to the debt dilemma is willful inflation. The Federal Reserve creates money on its own books and then purchases Treasury obligations. It does not matter much whether it buys new obligations directly from the Treasury or old obligations from sellers in the open market, who then may use the funds to bid for new issues. In both cases, the Fed purchases provide the funds that finance the deficits.

Inflation is a willful policy conducted by the central bank. It causes goods prices to rise and the purchasing power of money to decline; it depreciates all debt stated in monetary units. A ten percent rise in prices reduces the value of a $2.5 trillion federal debt pyramid by $250 billion. It may enable the Treasury to indulge in a deficit of $250 billion while it depreciates the debt pyramid by the same amount. Higher rates of inflation would visibly shrink the pyramid, while providing more funds to the U.S. Treasury. For a government deeply mired in debt, inflation offers an easy solution; moreover, it raises tax revenues and provides instant purchasing power for favorite programs.

In the coming storm, the federal government may be tempted to seek refuge with rampant inflation and debt depreciation. Yet, this possibility should probably be discounted for a number of reasons.

In the armory of debt depreciation and repudiation, it is a rather primitive method that is characterized by fiscal simplicity and crudity. American monetary authorities may be blinded and misguided by Keynesian thought, or they may be under the spell of supply-side magic or monetarist formulas, but they are not likely to embark upon willful monetary destruction. Neither Keynesian nor monetarist prescriptions call for double-digit inflation. Surely, our authorities may want to expand money and credit to the very limit of public acceptance and tolerance where rampant inflation raises its ugly head. Yet, at the abyss of monetary disorder, they are likely to reverse their course and return to more prudent methods. They did so in October of 1979, when a dollar crisis gripped foreign exchange markets, when the inflation rate exceeded fifteen percent, the prime rate stood at eighteen percent, the discount rate at thirteen percent plus three percent for central reserve city banks, when gold was about to soar to $800 an ounce and silver to $45. Frightened by the spectacle of looming disaster, the authorities got off the inflation accelerator and remained off for nearly two years. Experience keeps a dear school; the students may have learned their lessons.

Hyperinflation is a policy of desperados, such as the governments of Germany, Hungary, Poland, Russia, and China during and after a devastating war. It may also be the recipe of governments that are unable to exact more taxes from their subjects, although they are in urgent need of much revenue for the support of government-owned industries. Where government owns half of all facilities of production, as in Argentina, the need for revenue is always insatiable.

Rampant inflation is an unlikely course for American policy makers because the middle-class, which is the primary victim of inflation, is still existent and rather influential politically. It is practically the only social class whose members hold monetary savings and claims to money, such as pension funds, life insurances, annuities, and savings accounts. High rates of inflation would impoverish this important class in the span of a few years, which would generate vehement opposition and loud criticism. In a free society, the middle class, which constitutes the most numerous class at the polls, may still be heard in the halls of government and, therefore, be effective in calling a halt to monetary destruction. It takes a dictator and an army of gendarmes to silence the middle class and make off with its savings.

The possibility of chronic inflation at double-digit rates should also be discounted because the U.S. dollar is world money. Since the abolition of the gold standard in 1971, the U.S. dollar has become by far the world's most popular medium of exchange, held and used by countless millions of people around the globe. For U.S. monetary authorities to inflate this currency until the people dump it and shun it would require a degree of recklessness that is difficult to imagine. It would take trillions of dollars to generate new dollar crises such as those of 1978 and 1979, which would again call for a halt to such practices. It is difficult to imagine why U.S. authorities would want to risk the disintegration of a system that places them in the center of world finance, that exports their money to all corners of the world and permits Americans to import foreign goods in exchange for newly printed money. Why would they want to jeopardize the world dollar standard that permits Americans to live beyond their means? Unfortunately, politicians and officials do not think in such terms. For reasons difficult to fathom, they are talking about a currency reform that would exchange old dollars for new dollars. Such a reform that would seek to draw the money of the world to Washington for inspection and exchange, may indeed trigger a run from the dollar and the collapse of its purchasing power.

Acute Deflation

A few economists and financial advisors are convinced that, sooner or later, the U.S. financial structure will experience the very opposite of inflation, an acute deflation that will cause the United States to sink into a deep depression.[6] These "deflationists," just like the "inflationists," point at the sorry condition of the American banking system, especially the farm credit system. They call attention to the international situation that is so portentous. How, they ask, could the Fed cope with a wave of third world defaults and repudiations? They would overwhelm the Fed. The burden of debt is so heavy and the quality of much debt so poor that the debt pyramid is bound to crumble under its own weight. Bank failures will multiply in a chain reaction, and the stock of money will contract so rapidly that the Fed simply cannot keep up with its rescue operation. The shrinking quantity of money in turn will cause goods prices to fall and unemployment to rise in a scenario similar to that of the Great Depression.

The probability of this chain of events is probably smaller than that of hyperinflation. Deflationists underestimate the power of government. Judging present conditions by conditions and events in the past, they come to an old-fashioned conclusion: the Fed can stop a run on a single bank, but it cannot stop a run on several banks at the same time.

Actually, government can come to the rescue of any number of banks and financial institutions. The Federal Reserve can create new bank reserves with the speed of a computer command and transfer them in seconds by high speed modem; it can create $1 million as efficiently as it can create $1 billion or $100 billion and rush them to the banks under siege. It derives this vast power from its position as money monopolist and from the legal tender force of its money; both qualities were created by the U.S. Congress, are sanctioned by the courts, and enforced by the police.

The deflationists were correct under the gold standard, when all kinds of money were convertible into gold at a specified rate. Gold cannot be created at will, which limits the rescue powers of a central bank to its own gold reserves. Legal reserve requirements for its own notes and deposits further limit the central bank's ability to come to the rescue of insolvent commercial banks.

Deflationists are quick to point at the deflation of the early 1930s and the deep depression that engulfed economic activity everywhere. Unfortunately, they misinterpret the credit contraction and misread the lessons of the Great Depression. The contraction was not the result of human error and blunder on the part of Federal Reserve governors, as the would-be governors of monetarism are charging, but the inevitable consequence and by-product of the financial readjustment. A depression is a readjustment time when the factors of production are forced to readjust to the true state of the market, when bad investments are written down or written off. In a depression, the credit markets are forced to readjust to the actual supply of savings and the demand for savings. The credit contraction is a symptom of the readjustment process, it is not the cause of the depression.

Most economists are poor historians. They do not realize that the Great Depression did not spring from credit contraction; in reality, it was the inevitable consequence of the credit expansion that preceded the contraction, and of other unwise policies that compounded the difficulties. A great deal of blame for the depression must be placed on the disintegration of the world economy and the economic nationalism that eroded the world division of labor. The Hawley-Smoot Tariff Act of June, 1930, raised American tariffs to unprecedented levels, which practically closed American borders to foreign goods. Subsequently, protectionism ran wild over the world. Export industries fell into deep depression; unemployment grew with great rapidity. Farm prices in the United States dropped sharply thereafter. By 1932, even the most able farmer could no longer make ends meet.[7]

Historians also point at the Revenue Act of 1932, which doubled the income tax. In the midst of depression with more than 20 percent of Americans unemployed, Congress ordered the sharpest increase in federal exactions in American history. Exemptions were lowered, "earned income credit" was eliminated. Normal tax rates were raised from a range of 1½–5 percent to 4–8 percent, surtax rates from 20 percent to 55 percent. Estate taxes were boosted and gift taxes were imposed with rates from ¾ percent to 33½ percent. In short, the Hoover Administration nearly doubled the burden of government during the depression, which alone would bring any economy to its knees.[8]

When President Franklin Delano Roosevelt came to power, new rules, regulations, and taxes struck hard at the profitability of commerce and industry. The New Deal managed to prolong the depression with a great number of anti-revival measures. The National Industrial Recovery Act sought to increase purchasing power by increasing payrolls. Confiscation of the people's gold holdings and subsequently dollar devaluation sought to stimulate foreign buying. The Agricultural Adjustment Act sought to raise farm income by cutting the acreage planted or destroying the crops in the fields, and by paying farmers not to plant certain crops. The National Labor Relations Act took labor out of the courts of law and lodged it in a newly created federal agency, the National Labor Relations Board. The law led to thousands of strikes that forced millions of workers into the union fold. Ugly sit-down strikes shut down hundreds of plants and pushed business into deep depression. Individual enterprise, the only mainspring of prosperity, just did not have a chance. It is simplistic and crude to lay the blame for the Great Depression on the Fed credit contraction of 1931 and 1932.[9]

Strict Regulation

A deep depression like the Great Depression is unlikely to engulf us without the combination of factors that brought it about. Although the old factors continue to be at work with varying intensity, they do not point toward prolonged deflation and deep depression, but rather at a highly regimented economy. Government intervention is too pervasive and political power too potent to permit any one scenario. The most likely course of events points toward comprehensive regulation and control, and a full array of economic consequences. The blunders of the 1980s in expanding the political transfer system and permitting it to consume productive capital en masse may bring forth the strict regulation and regimentation of the 1990s, especially in financial matters.

The particular form of regimentation may depend on the crisis that will usher it in. A crisis in foreign-investor confidence may invite a different reaction from a third world debtor default, or from a deepening depression, a crushing interest burden, paralyzing protectionism, or the threat of economic radicalism. Whatever it may be, the financial institutions laboring under a heavy burden of debt may be unable to carry out their expected functions. They may not be in a position to expand credit fast enough to stimulate the sagging economy, or give prompt relief to domestic and foreign debtors. To prevent a worsening crisis, the federal government may provide relief and support to ever widening circles of financial institutions, and subsequently place them under tight supervision and control. In the end, the level of government involvement may be greater than ever before.

Under dire conditions of national emergency, the federal government would want to reorganize and restructure the pyramid of debt. It may embark upon an "interest reduction" and "debt conversion" policy, which would necessitate complete control over the credit industry. The Federal Reserve System would probably be nationalized, that is, legal ownership be placed with the federal government. Its structure and function would remain unchanged. All private credit institutions would be nationalized in the economic sense, that is, be tightly regulated and controlled, although the legal titles remain with the owners. In short order, laws and regulations would mandate conversion of foreign debts, followed by conversions of municipal and state obligations and, finally, federal debts. Average interest rates on long-term public debt would be slashed from more than eight percent to some four percent. The large volume of short-term obligations of the U.S. Treasury would be converted to a four percent "liberty bond loan," redeemable in 25 years, which may correspond with the maturity and yield of the restructured municipal debt. A law or regulation pertaining to private credits and loans may reduce interest rates on mortgages and mortgage bonds to five to six percent. Savings banks and insurance companies would be expected to set a shining example.

A financial crisis can be expected to lead to a painful increase in taxation, which would likely be hidden by a dense veil of public regulation and control. Numerous new government authorities may come into existence, imposing new payment liabilities that do not appear on tax ledgers, but are taxes nevertheless. Middle and especially higher income producers may suffer significant tax boosts; business taxes may be raised substantially. In one form or another, government may extract another twenty to twenty-five percent of national income from the working population.

The U.S. dollar may become a managed currency with multiple exchange rates. When frightened foreign investors withdraw their funds, causing severe stringencies in U.S. markets, the federal government may block their accounts, which would create a number of different U.S. dollars selling at various discounts. All foreign exchange in American hands may have to be sold to the Federal Reserve, acting as the monopolistic buyer. Conversely, the Fed may become the sole seller of foreign exchange and, as such, sit in judgment of all foreign payments. It may allocate foreign funds for "justifiable" purchases and deny payment for "nonessential" goods and services. It may seize control over financial markets to block the flight of American capital from the United States and facilitate the repayment of foreign capital "in an orderly fashion." To restore the balance of payments, federal authorities may redirect, as far as possible, the importation of goods from surplus countries, such as Japan and West Germany, to deficit countries that buy more from the United States than they are selling, such as most third world countries.

In the end, the federal government debt will be repaid and the balance of payments restored; Treasury obligations will be paid through "roll-overs" at half the contract rate of interest, which will reduce their market value by a corresponding percentage. Inflation is likely to depreciate the balance at various rates after taxation takes its bite. Whatever is left may be converted to 25-year bonds, or be placed in blocked accounts.

Great changes are bound to come. The end of the deficit era is coming in sight; the payment era is likely to follow. Indeed, it must follow. To live beyond our means today is to live below them tomorrow.

11

ETERNAL HOPE

A Moral Standard

We are never beneath hope; in all things, it is better to hope than to despair. In the political world, much can be done if man changes his mind and brings a thorough will to do it. There is no inevitability in the coming of inflation, deflation, or regimentation. Man makes laws and repeals them. He has made laws that are sowing the seeds of conflict and strife; he can repeal them. He has enacted laws that are promising to do what laws cannot do; he can rescind them. Man may live above his circumstances, or decide to live within his means. He may indulge in deficit spending or balance his budget; there are no uncontrollable expenditures, no unavoidable deficits.

He who reforms himself is doing much to reform others. Reform, like charity, must begin at home. Once accomplished at home, it will radiate outward, kindle new light, and spread in geometric proportion. The true reformer is a seminal reformer, not a radical. He does not pass laws that mandate the reformation of others. He himself makes a beginning and does not think of himself as a reformer. The world may reject him as odd, impractical, and even irrational; but he clings to his principles, regardless of the world around him. There is boldness, a spirit of daring, in the heart of a reformer.

Significant reforms, in the final analysis, are moral reforms, changes in the perception of right conduct. Certain moral standards are basic to social order: sanctity of human life and dignity of the individual. They may not change much from one generation to the next. Other standards may undergo visible changes in the span of one generation or two, such as individual independence and self-reliance; the ethos of labor; thrift, honesty, and integrity; and respect for private property. Changes in these standards lead to changes in the system of economic and social organization. In this century, they sowed the seeds of economic and social conflict, and paved the way for political intervention in our lives. They gave birth to a transfer and entitlement system that is eroding the private property order. A reform that would restore it and remove the transfer predilection would have to restore the harmony of interests and repair the moral standards. It would have to rebuild the economic order on the old foundation of the Eighth Commandment—Thou shalt not steal—and of the Tenth— Thou shalt not covet anything that is thy neighbor's.

Breaching the Strongholds

To reconstruct a moral order is to set shining examples in the very strongholds of the political transfer system.[1] Reconstruction would have to begin with Social Security and Medicare, the most expensive and imposing bastions of the system, formidable and intimidating to all reformers. They are the very pillars of the transfer system; to exempt them from review and render them untouchable is to leave the system untouched. To exempt them from budget restraint when massive deficits are suffered and other programs are cut is to reaffirm the very transfer system. The Reagan Administration reconfirmed the Roosevelt Social Security system and the Johnson Medicare system when it not only rendered them untouchable and uncontrollable, but also reinforced them with "catastrophic insurance" and "nursing care."

It is difficult to castigate the transfer system with economic arguments. Surely, economists can point out that political transfer breeds economic and social conflict, that it reduces labor productivity and income, and that, in the end, it weakens and impoverishes the transfer society. All these effects are subject to explanation and interpretation; the causes can be explained away and the effects may actually be used to justify more political transfer. Growing poverty may bring forth ever more government intervention seeking to alleviate poverty. Moreover, economic arguments deploring "lack of funds" and "red-ink spending" are likely to be counterproductive. To point at empty pockets and treasuries in the sight of much wealth and luxury all around us does not ring true. It is utterly ineffective against passionate descriptions of human need and want. Yet, the most common criticism leveled at the transfer system is "we cannot afford it." It leaves the moral argument for transfer and entitlement completely unanswered; instead, it initiates a search for funds that make it affordable. In the end, the funds are promptly secured through higher taxes on young people, or deficit financing that consumes their savings.

Social Security

It is futile to point at the costs of the Social Security System. More than nine out of ten workers (126 million) pay more than $227 billion a year so that some forty million retired or disabled people and their dependents may receive monthly Social Security checks. They pay more than $82 billion so that over twenty-three million people, 65 and over, nearly all of the nation's older population, draw health care benefits under Medicare; another three million disabled people under 65 enjoy the same benefits. Obviously, every American has a stake in Social Security, either as a beneficiary or as a victim, or both.[2]

It is a formidable system built on political expedience and political immorality. It exacts income and wealth from one social class to enrich another. It keeps on growing and shifting an ever growing burden on the working people. Sooner or later the victims may resent the shifting and endeavor to lighten their load through realistic reductions in benefits or outright repudiation. They may want to abolish the System because it is the product of politics, very popular with politicians and their beneficiaries, and yet so grossly unjust and unethical. The reform generation may want to halt the feverish efforts at transfer, and liquidate the System proceeding along the following lines:[3]

Information to Recipients. To restore a commonplace truth and realism, every recipient of Social Security benefits should be informed of the nature and source of his benefits. Every check should carry a stub that reveals the dollar amount contributed to the System by him and his employer, and the cumulative amount of benefits received by him as of that check. The stub should show that he or she contributed a total of $817.15 and, as of now, withdrew $69,501.15. Such shocking revelation would soon silence the most common defense: "I paid in."

Means Test. When the total benefits received in retirement exceed the contributions made during the productive years, the recipient should undergo a means test. Anyone who can cover his own expenses should be expected to do so. Millionaires and other affluent retirees should be expected to pay their own bills. A poor retiree who is lacking the means of support may seek public assistance. He is getting it now, but calling it "Social Security."

Parent and Child. When public assistance seems to be called for, the children of a retired worker should be given an opportunity to contribute to the support of their parents. As parents are responsible for their children, so are children responsible for their parents. No Social Security System should eradicate this moral law and Biblical Commandment.

Conscientious Objectors. The System should not violate the religious and moral principles of conscientious objectors. Even in such a vital matter as national defense, American society has always respected the principles of those Americans who refused to bear arms or participate in military service. The same respect should be accorded to all religious and moral objectors to Social Security.

Relief for Young Workers. To grant relief to the primary victims of the System and abate the frantic shifting of burdens to future generations, we should seek to protect our youth by limiting its losses. To this end, it is proposed that no one should be forced to remain in the System. Anyone willing to assume self-responsibility for his old age and his medical expenses should be permitted to do so.

The financial dilemma of the Social Security System is giving rise to numerous reform proposals. Many turn out to be new concoctions of the same old redistribution medicine, prescribing new victims for old beneficiaries. In contrast, these proposals begin with truth and information, which are the seeds for a true reform, and build on moral conduct, rather than political expedience. Reformation is a work of time. We must rebuild and regenerate moral awareness, which in time will bring forth genuine reform.

Medicare

In the meantime, it is time to brace ourselves for another financial crisis: the crisis of Medicare.[4] When the U.S. Congress is not coping with Social Security losses, it is struggling with Medicare deficits. Just recently, it was facing staggering Social Security deficits that were estimated at $180 billion over a seven-year period; now the budget office is warning us of a $310 billion accumulated Medicare deficit by 1995. It is clear that the Health Insurance Fund is in serious financial trouble. In fact, it is facing insolvency within four years, unless Congress finds a way to raise revenue or control soaring medical expenditures.

The dilemma of Medicare is a dangerous political issue. At any moment, it may explode into a partisan fracas such as the bitter confrontations on Social Security. Vying for the votes of the elderly, the political parties may again accuse each other of callous disregard of decency, responsibility, and morality. Surely, in the end they can be expected to cooperate again by raising the tax levies on some hapless taxpayers. The question of morality then will be shelved until such time as Medicare needs to be rescued again.

To many observers, Medicare is an unfailing index of political immorality. Born from the transfer entitlement mentality in the 1960s, fostered by political power and government force, nourished by tax collectors and IRS agents, Medicare is a creature of politics. It takes income and wealth from some people to finance the medical bills of other people. It rests on brute political force that uses the instruments of government to benefit one social class at the expense of other classes.

According to all financial analyses, the distribution of personal wealth is directly proportional to the age of the individual. Young people, as a class, are much poorer than old people, most of whom managed to accumulate some measure of material comfort and wealth. Unfortunately, transfer policies are rarely guided by considerations of comfort and wealth; they are determined by political power and popular majority, which places youth at a distinct disadvantage in the political process. The elderly manage to vote themselves benefit entitlements and allocate the costs to younger people. They work through Medicare, which seizes income and wealth from the poorer classes, and bestows free medical benefits on their own.

The very existence of Medicare raises difficult questions of political morality. Is it moral for a political majority to seize income and wealth from one social class, in this case the younger, poorer population, to benefit another social class? Is it right to use the apparatus of government to benefit one social class at the expense of others? Is it proper and just to establish permanent transfer agencies that redistribute income and wealth?

The moral question of Medicare raises many questions of individual conscience and behavior. Is it proper, fair, and moral for an individual to partake of the transfer benefits derived by political force? Someone's Medicare benefit is always a painful financial exaction from someone else. Is it moral for anyone to inflict such pains on others? In particular, the dear old lady in mink with a six-figure bank account, is she acting morally when she inflicts the Medicare pains on young people by claiming her benefits? The Medicare card in the pocket of an heiress to the Rockefeller, Ford, or Mellon fortune, is it not a glaring badge of political immorality? Is it not such a badge in *anyone's* pocket?

What are we to think of an affluent family whose aging mother depends for her medical needs on government and Medicare? What are we to think of sons and daughters who deliver their parents to Medicare? How are we to judge a Medicare society?

We may not find fault with the doctor who serves Medicare patients unless he becomes a spokesman and promoter of the system. After all, a doctor who is providing healthcare services to the sick and needy cannot be expected to search into the sources of the money he receives in exchange. He may even specialize in and concentrate on services rendered to Medicare patients because there is a profitable demand. Yet, he should not be faulted as long as he does not promote it, he himself does not use it or urge his mother to use it. We may even applaud him when he reminds the dear-old-lady patient in mink of the poor taxpayers who are forced to pay her bills.

Many critics of the Medicare system are questioning its medical effectiveness and cost efficiency. They are lamenting the health-cost inflation and are searching for solutions. They rarely raise the crucial question of political morality. Should an immoral system be made more effective and cost-efficient, or should it be reformed along the lines of Judeo-Christian morality? Can the cost issue ever be resolved without first solving the moral issue?

The federal government must be extricated from the health care business. To allow politicians and bureaucrats in any business is to inject political immorality. After all, most politicians make decisions on the basis of popular majority, rather than morality. They take polls, rather than reflect on basic principles of morality. Unfortunately, opinion polls provide no guidepost for questions of morality.

Medicare reformers are concerned about the special interests in the health care industry that make it the special target of politics. Surely, in the lives of most people, food, clothing, and shelter are more important than medical care. Most of the time, they are more important also in the lives of the elderly. To sustain human life, the farmer, butcher, baker, textile worker, carpenter, plumber, and many others are as indispensable as the doctor and nurse. Why should health care of the elderly be singled out and be regulated and controlled by politicians?

Medicare critics applaud anyone's effort to force Medicare cuts through Congress. They favor all efforts to trim costs by raising premiums and "co-payments," the share of the health care burden borne by Medicare recipients. In particular, they are demanding a "means test" that would eliminate the most glaring cases of political immorality, the Medicare cards issued to millionaires and billionaires, and all others who are more able to pay their medical bills than young people. They would extend the means test also to the children of the elderly claiming Medicare and Medicaid benefits. Why should affluent sons and daughters not be expected to cover the medical bills of their needy parents?

When children abandon the care of their parents to government and its institutions, both suffer tragic losses. Most of all, the children lose their possibility of growth in being human and moral. In days to come, their iniquities will be visited upon them as their children imitate them.

What the critics of the system are unable to accomplish through information and education, the AIDS virus may achieve in less than a decade.[5] It is devastating the government health care system. Some three to four million Americans are presently infected by the dread disease, and every ten to twelve months, the number of AIDS patients is doubling. If it continues to double every year, 64 million Americans are estimated to be infected by the end of 1990, just three years from now. Health officials expect that one million patients will soon die every year, and ten million in 2000. With just 1,260,000 hospital beds available in the United States, the hospitals are likely to be crowded. At the present, AIDS patients are staying an average of 167 days in the hospital before they die, at an expense of some $147,000 per patient. In the year 2000, if no cure is found, it will take nearly $1.5 trillion to nurse them until they die.

The immoral transfer system places the financial burden on Medicare and Medicaid. The dying call out for Medicaid to bear their medical expenses; the survivors of the deceased who worked under Social Security for at least 1½ years in the 3 years before death qualify for Social Security survivor benefits. No matter what dollar amounts the system may exact from its working people, the revenue will be grossly insufficient to cover the AIDS health care demand.

In ages gone, when moral obligation meant conformity to the will of God, carriers of contagious diseases who knowingly and willfully infected other individuals, and thereby inflicted great suffering and early death on others, would have been treated as criminals, yea, even as murderers, and been promptly quarantined from the healthy community. The transfer society, in contrast, is jealously safeguarding the civil rights of AIDS carriers who may infect others with criminal immunity; it is eagerly loading the financial burden of their care on working survivors, and squarely placing politicians and officials in charge of it all. A mysterious death wish seems to drive the transfer society; the AIDS epidemic may make it come true.

A Spending Freeze

The critics of the transfer order draw an important distinction between political intervention that is continuously misdirecting economic activity and hampering economic production, such as all forms of price and wage controls, and that intervention which benefits one class of people at the expense of another. The former must be abolished without delay, the latter in an orderly fashion.

The strongholds of the American transfer system, Social Security and Medicare, must be dismantled in an orderly fashion. The beneficiaries must be made aware of the nature of their benefits, and be placed on notice that the transfer process will be terminated. The first step in this direction must be a spending freeze that calls a truce to the political struggle.

In reaction to popular criticism, a few politicians have made deficit reduction proposals, and even urged spending freezes, to meet certain deficit targets. Spending does not need to be cut, taxes need not be raised, they inform us, expenditures must be frozen until the natural growth in revenues catches up with the spending. If expenditures are kept constant for a while, the budget deficit will shrink and eventually disappear.

Senator Pete Domenici of New Mexico recently proposed that Congress freeze Fiscal Year 1988 budget authority at Fiscal Year 1987 spending levels.[6] Federal spending in 1987 is estimated at $1 trillion, revenues at $850 billion. Revenues are estimated to rise to $933 in FY 1988, to $996 in 1989, and $1.058 trillion in 1990. If expenditures were frozen at 1987 levels until 1990, the federal budget would be in the black.

The Domenici proposal, like so many other deficit reduction proposals, attacks the symptoms instead of the disease. Surely, it points at the high growth rate of spending and urges temporary moderation until receipts catch up with outlays. Unfortunately, it does not in the least touch upon the root cause of the evil, the transfer mentality, which generates outlays faster than revenue can be collected. The Domenici proposal holds out new hope for more benefits in 1990 when surpluses would be expected. While it deplores the red ink, it implicitly welcomes the transfer accounts.

It is significant that the Domenici freeze would exempt government pay increases and Congressional salary raises. If it is true that example is more forcible than precept, the Domenici exemption is likely to be more persuasive than the proposal. To an outside observer, political objectives present inscrutable puzzles of intent, design, and sincerity.

A New Beginning

A world is a scene of changes. Conditions will either get better or grow worse; they are unlikely to remain the same for long. Pessimists, who instinctively take the gloomiest possible view of a situation, are holding to the belief that all things ultimately tend toward evil. They are preparing for ever larger fiscal debts and deficits, followed by soaring inflation and deteriorating levels of living. They are convinced that a society that is preoccupied with entitlement and depredation cannot remain free for long. Pessimists take a dim view of optimists who, observing the present trend, may not deny the ultimate destination of the transfer road, but expect society soon to take another road. With their disposition to expect the best possible outcome, optimists dwell on the most hopeful aspects of the situation. Trust men, they assure us, and they will be true in the end; expect greatness and they will show themselves great. Trust America, it will remain the home of freedom and the hope of the world.

Changes in human affairs are the work of changes in moral standards. The American transfer system, with all its political power, is an elaborate product of contemporary standards. It is changing continually, as the public perception of right conduct is changing, which wields more power than the U.S. Congress and a thousand judges. Changes are cosmopolitan, sweeping across national boundaries, affecting human affairs everywhere. Governments cannot prevent them; they may smother them and coercion may suppress them temporarily, but nothing can prevent them for long.

American economic conditions may deteriorate because false ideas may guide the body politic towards stagnation and disintegration; but conditions elsewhere may improve rapidly because economic policies are guided by inexorable economic law. They may deteriorate slowly in the United States and improve visibly in Japan, Hong Kong, or Singapore. They may deteriorate in Mexico, but improve in Argentina, always in direct proportion to man's moral order. When economic conditions are improving elsewhere while they are deteriorating in the United States, the American people may repent of their ways and return to the proven road. The success of more prosperous societies may set the example.

The American people may remember someday that, to sustain human life and well-being, they must labor. Income and wealth are the fruits of individual effort and service; to extract them from each other by political force is both immoral and counterproductive. Political largesse raises an army of idle beneficiaries, promotes consumption without production, and discourages effort and thrift. Transfer income by political force is worse than no income at all. The transfer state openly and officially hampers economic output. It may erect production barriers, impose tariffs and quotas, parity prices, and acreage restrictions; it may resort to inflation, credit expansion, and deficit spending. It tends to be self-destructive.

An American Freedom Party may some day put an end to political intervention designed to favor half the population at the expense of the other half and to reduce the supply of goods and render them more expensive. An organization of persons united for the purpose of influencing government policy toward greater economic well-being may signal the end of the transfer system. Although recent history contains many sordid and selfish chapters, political parties may be powerful forces for good in a free society. A Freedom Party may educate and organize public opinion by keeping the people informed on the follies of policies restricting output, reducing supplies, and benefiting some voters at the expense of others. It may contribute to civic education, present candidates for public offices, and serve to represent millions of Americans who are interested in rising standards of living and lower goods prices.

Many American voters are women who are homemakers and mothers. It is difficult to believe that, if they were informed, they would cast their votes for benefits and bounty for themselves and debts for their children. American women are the natural members of the Freedom Party that opposes policies designed to restrict production, to raise prices, and to favor one social class at the expense of another. Young people who are vitally interested in the preservation of the apparatus of production are their natural allies. The present system has made youth the primary beast of burden and victim of transfer; the most monstrous burdens, Social Security and Medicare, have been placed squarely on the shoulders of youth. An American Freedom Party would show mercy and promptly remove the horrid load.

No affliction nor temptation should induce us to despair. It is necessary to hope, for hope itself is happiness and the beginning of reform.

NOTES

Chapter 1. *The Politics of Deficit Spending*

[1] *Budget of the United States Government*, Fiscal Year 1987, pp. 6e-45.

[2] *The Wall Street Journal*, February 11, 1986, pp. 1, 27.

[3] *Facts and Figures on Government Finance*, 23rd ed. (Washington, DC: Tax Foundation, Inc., 1986), p. a25.

[4] Ron Paul, *Freedom Report*, (Lake Jackson, TX: Jan. 1983).

[5] Randall Fitzgerald and Gerald Lipson, *Pork Barrel*, (Washington, DC: Cato Institute, 1984).

[6] *Ibid.*, p. xviii.

[7] Foreword to *Pork Barrel*, p. viii.

[8] Ludwig von Mises, *Bureaucracy*, 1944 (Spring Mills, PA: Libertarian Press, Inc., 1983).

Chapter 2. *Income by Majority Vote*

[1] John Stuart Mill, *Principles of Political Economy*, 5th edition (New York: D. Appleton and Co., 1894), pp. 40–41.

[2] Karl Marx, *Capital*, from the third German edition (London, William Glaisher, Ltd., 1912), pp. 365–366; cf. also Part III, "The Production of Absolute Surplus-Value," pp. 156–363.

[3] *The Budget of the United States Government*, Fiscal Year, 1987, pp. 3-9, 6, 6d-131. *Special Analyses*, Fiscal Year 1986, p. b-12.

[4] Hans F. Sennholz, *Social Security—Is Reform Possible?* (Grove City, PA: PPE Fund, Inc., 1981).

[5] *The Budget of the United States Government*, Fiscal Year 1987, pp. 3-10, 5-91, 5-94, 6d-257.

[6] Tax Foundation, Inc., Washington, DC: *Facts and Figures in Government Finance*, 1986, pp. d8, d46.

[7] *Ibid.* p. d47.

[8] Rousas J. Rushdoony, *Intellectual Schizophrenia* (Philadelphia, PA: The Presbyterian and Reformed Publishing Company, 1971), pp. 63–65.

[9] George Grant, *Bringing in the Sheaves* (Atlanta, GA: American Vision Press, 1985), p. 46.

[10]   Clarence B. Carson, *The War on the Poor* (New Rochelle, NY: Arlington House, 1969); Walter E. Williams, *The State Against Blacks*, (New York, NY: McGraw-Hill, 1982); Thomas Sowell, *Civil Rights: Rhetoric or Reality?* (New York, NY: William Morrow and Co., 1984); Martin Anderson, *Welfare* (Stanford, CA: Hoover Institution Press, 1978).

[11]   *The Budget of the United States Government*, Fiscal Year 1987, p. 5-51.

[12]   *Ibid.*, p. 5-50.

[13]   *Ibid.*, pp. 5-19, 5-23.

[14]   P. T. (Lord) Bauer, *Third World and Economic Delusion* (London: Methuen, 1981).

[15]   *The Budget of the United States Government*, Fiscal Year 1987, pp. 5-2, 5-153.

Chapter 3. *The Ethics of Entitlement*

[1]   Arthur C. Pigou, *Economics of Welfare* (London: Macmillan, 4th ed., 1932), p. 89.

[2]   Aba P. Lerner, *The Economics of Control* (New York: Macmillan, 3rd ed. 1947), Chap. II, p. 29.

[3]   *Ibid.*, pp. 29–32.

[4]   Jonathan Hughes, *The Vital Few* (New York: Oxford University Press, 1986), p. 121 *et seq.*

Chapter 4. *Underground Government*

[1]   Cf. James T. Bennett and Thomas J. DiLorenzo, *Underground Government: The Off-Budget Public Sector* (Washington, DC: Cato Institute, 1983), p. 4 *et seq.*

[2]   Pennsylvania Department of Community Affairs, *Directory of Municipal Authorities in Pennsylvania—1984* (Harrisburg: Department of Community Affairs, 1984), Statistics, pp. 9–11.

[3]   *Facts and Figures on Government Finance*, 23rd edition (Washington, DC: Tax Foundation, 1986), p. f29. Data as of the end of fiscal year 1983.

[4]   *Ibid.*

[5]   *Ibid.* p. e61. Data as of end of fiscal year 1983. Projection of a five year trend permits an estimate of some $160 billion nonguaranteed debt in 1986, amounting to some 70 percent of total New York State indebtedness.

6 James T. Bennett and Thomas J. DiLorenzo, *ibid.*, pp. 60–68.

7 New York is followed by California with a state debt of $12 billion, New Jersey $10.3 billion, Illinois $7.8 billion, Massachusetts $7.4 billion. *Facts and Figures on Government Finance*, pp. e62, e63.

8 *Budget of the United States Government*, Fiscal Year 1986, p. 6–11.

9 *Special Analyses, Budget of the United States Government*, Fiscal Year 1986, p. f-42.

10 *Special Analyses*, p. f-23.

11 *Special Analyses*, p. f-20.

12 Cf. Ludwig von Mises, *Bureaucracy* (Spring Mills, PA: Libertarian Press, 1983).

13 James T. Bennett and Thomas J. DiLorenzo, *ibid.*, p. 125.

Chapter 5. *Deficits Do Matter*

1 Hans F. Sennholz, *Age of Inflation* (Belmont, MA: Western Islands, 1979), p. 109 *et seq.*; also *Inflation or Gold Standard* (Lansing, MI: Bramble Minibook, 1973). Under the influence of Keynesian thought, many economists defend government debt on grounds of "the fallacy of composition." What is true for individuals may be false for the whole of society. "Why do conservatives complain about the size of the public debt?" asks Paul A. Samuelson. They fall prey to an old myth, the fallacy of composition. Cf. *Economics*, 12th edition (New York: McGraw-Hill Book Co.) p. 360.

2 "Only external debt is like individual debt and impoverishes the nation," says Aba P. Lerner. Cf. his *Economics of Control* (New York: The Macmillan Company, 1944) p. 305 *et seq.* For a cogent refutation cf. James M. Buchanan, *The Public Finances* (Homewood, IL: Richard D. Irwin, Inc., 1965), p. 379.

3 *Special Analyses, Budget of the United States Government, 1987*, p. e-15.

4 Paul L. Poirot, "The Size of the National Debt Doesn't Matter Because We Owe It to Ourselves," in *Clichés of Socialism*, #6 (Irvington-on-Hudson, NY: The Foundation for Economic Education, Inc., 1956).

5 Cf. Hans F. Sennholz, *The Politics of Unemployment* (Spring Mills, PA: Libertarian Press, 1987).

6 Cf. Jude Wanniski, *The Way the World Works* (New York: Simon and Schuster, 1978), p. 160; Jack Kemp, the political leader of the supply-side movement, prefers to ignore the problems of federal

indebtedness. Cf. his *An American Renaissance* (New York: Harper & Row, 1979).

[7] *Budget of the United States Government, 1987*, p. 5-155.

Chapter 6. *Worse Than 1929*

[1] Benjamin M. Anderson, *Economics and the Public Welfare* (New York: D. Van Nostrand, 1949), p. 113.

[2] *Ibid.*, p. 195.

[3] *Conference Board Economic Record*, March 20, 1940, cited by Benjamin M. Anderson, *ibid.*, p. 488.

[4] *Federal Reserve Bulletin*, May 1987, p. a13.

[5] *Ibid.*, p. a51.

[6] Jeffrey M. Laderman, "What the Rally Really Means" in *Business Week* (A McGraw-Hill Publication), February 2, 1987, pp. 58–60.

[7] *Ibid.*, p. 60.

[8] Paul Craig Roberts, "Reaganomics: Bad Press or No, It Works," in *Business Week*, January 26, 1987, p. 24.

[9] Jeffrey M. Laderman, *ibid.*, p. 59.

[10] Alfred L. Malabre, Jr., *Beyond Our Means* (New York: Random House, 1987), pp. 124–129, 140–143. The author astutely points at the extraordinarily high compensation of top executives in banking and other industries. While they are turning to Washington for help of various sorts and pressing their employees to hold the line, American executives are raising their pay by leaps and bounds. It is at least twice that of their foreign counterparts. The reason for this embarrassing development undoubtedly can be traced to the fact that American inheritance and income taxation has greatly reduced or even eliminated family ownership, and thereby delivered the control of corporations to "professional" managers. Owning few or no shares at all, their primary concern is their own salaries, fringes, and perks.

Chapter 7. *Palliatives and Panaceas*

[1] Stephen Moore, editor, *Slashing the Deficit, Fiscal Year 1987* (Washington, DC: The Heritage Foundation), pp. ix–x; cf. also Steve H. Hanke, *Privatization: Theory, Evidence, and Implementation* (Washington, DC: The Ludwig von Mises Institute, 1986).

[2] Stephen Moore, *Ibid.*, p. x.

[3] *Ibid.*, p. xviii.

4   *Budget of the United States Government, Fiscal Year 1986* (Washington, DC).

5   Congressional Budget Office, *Curtailing Indirect Federal Subsidies to the U.S. Postal Service*, August, 1984.

6   *Budget of the United States Government, Ibid*, p. 5-93.

7   Gottfried Dietze, *America's Political Dilemma* (Baltimore, MD: Johns Hopkins Press, 1968), pp. 22, 27, 38–41, 183–187.

8   Cf. above, pp. 43–54

9   President Ronald Reagan, Senators Strom Thurmond (R-SC) and Orrin Hatch (R-UT) are the chief sponsors of the amendment.

10   The eighteen states that did not pass a balanced-budget resolution are: California, Connecticut, Hawaii, Illinois, Kentucky, Maine, Massachusetts, Michigan, Minnesota, Montana, New Jersey, New York, Ohio, Rhode Island, Vermont, Washington, West Virginia, Wisconsin.

11   Organized labor, led by the AFL-CIO and the American Federation of State, County and Municipal Employees (AFSCME), along with senior citizens' groups ardently oppose the amendment. Senators Charles McC. Mathias, Jr., (R-MD), and Max Baucus, (D-MT) lead the Congressional opposition. Cf. *Congressional Quarterly*, 99th Congress, 2nd Session, 1986 (Washington, DC: *Congressional Quarterly, Inc.*), p. 578; also 97th Congress, 2nd Session, 1982, p. 392.

12   *Congressional Quarterly Almanac*, 1985, pp. 468, 469.

13   Jude Wanniski, *The Way the World Works* (New York: Simon and Schuster, 1978), p. 97 *et seq*; Arthur B. Laffer, Memo to U.S. Treasury Secretary William Simon, November 1974; Jack Kemp, *The Tax Bill is a Mistake* (Encyclopedia Americana & CBS News: Audio Resource Library, 1982); also *An American Renaissance* (New York: Harper & Row, 1979).

14   *Budget of the United States Government, Fiscal Year 1987*, pp. 5-86, 103, 113, 127, 132.

15   Cf. above, pp. 55–69.

Chapter 8. *Taxes and Tributes*

1   Adam Smith, *An Inquiry Into the Nature and Causes of The Wealth of Nations*, 1776, The Modern Library, ed. by Edwin Canaan (New York: Random House, Inc. 1965), p. 878.

2   F. A. Hayek, *The Constitution of Liberty* (Chicago, IL: The University of Chicago Press, 1960), p. 312.

[3]   Ron Paul, "Taxes and Deficits" in *Freedom Report*, Vol. IX, No. 2, (Lake Jackson, TX: Foundation for Rational Economics and Education, Inc., 1985), p. 1.

[4]   *U.S. Code, Congressional and Administrative News*, 99th Congress, First Session, 1985 (St. Paul, MN: West Publishing Co., 1985), Vol. 1, December 12, 1985; also Vol. 2, pp. 979–1054; *Congressional Quarterly Almanac*, Vol. XVI, 1985 (Washington, DC: Congressional Quarterly, Inc.), pp. 459–468.

[5]   *Budget of the United States Government*, Fiscal Year 1987, p. 6e-47.

Chapter 9. *A Letter to the President*

[1]   The writer arrived at this amount by estimating the market value of the fringe benefits described below.

[2]   Joseph Nathan Kane, *Facts About the Presidents* (New York: The H. W. Wilson Co., 1981), pp. 417–418.

[3]   *Budget of the United States Government, 1987*, p. 6d-25.

Chapter 10. *The Coming Storm*

[1]   *The Budget of the United States Government*, Fiscal Year 1987, p. m-5.

[2]   *Dollars & Sense*, Vol. 17, No. 2, March 1986 (Washington, DC: National Taxpayers Union), p. 5.

[3]   Alfred L. Malabre, Jr., *Beyond Our Means* (New York: Random House, 1987), p. 133.

[4]   *Ibid*, p. 155.

[5]   *The Budget of the United States Government*, Fiscal Year 1987, p. m-2.

[6]   Julian Snyder of *International Moneyline* and many other deflationists base their deliberations on the writings of the Soviet economist N. D. Kondratieff, who sought to prove the presence of "long waves" as characteristic of the capitalistic order. Several economists and many financial writers draw their conclusions from these waves.

[7]   Cf. Hans F. Sennholz, *The Great Depression* (Lansing, MI: Constitutional Alliance, Inc., 1969).

[8]   *Ibid*, p. 15.

[9]   Benjamin M. Anderson, *Economics and the Public Welfare* (New York: D. Van Nostrand Company, Inc., 1949), p. 263.

Chapter 11. *Eternal Hope*

1   Cf. above, p. 23–42.

2   Peter J. Ferrara explores important philosophical questions in his *Social Security* (Washington, DC: Cato Institute, 1980); he also edited *Social Security, Prospects for Real Reform*, which is an up-to-date analysis of the continuing problems of the System (Washington, DC: Cato Institute, 1985); cf. also Douglas Brown, *An American Philosophy of Social Security* (Princeton, NJ: Princeton University Press, 1972); Edwin E. Witte, *The Development of the Social Security Act* (Madison, WI: The University of Wisconsin Press, 1972); Joseph A. Pechman, Henry J. Aaron, and Michael K. Taussig, *Social Security: Perspectives for Reform* (Washington, DC: Brookings Institution, 1968); Alicia H. Munnell, *The Future of Social Security* (Washington, DC: Brookings Institution, 1977).

3   Cf. Hans F. Sennholz, *Social Security, Is Reform Possible?* (Grove City, PA: Public Policy Education Funds, Inc., 1981).

4   Hans F. Sennholz, "Another Federal Catastrophe," *Private Practice* (Shawnee, OK: CCMS Publishing Co.), Vol. 18, No. 4, April 1986, p. 21 *et seq*; John C. Goodman, *The Regulation of Medical Care: Is the Price Too High?* (Washington, DC: Cato Institute, 1980).

5   *Congressional Quarterly, Almanac*, 99th Congress, 2nd Session, 1986 (Washington, DC: Congressional Quarterly Inc.), pp. 258, 261; cf. also Cheryl Russell on the fear of AIDS ending the sexual revolution, *The Wall Street Journal*, March 30, 1987, p. 18; Gary North, "The Plague Has Come at Last," *Remnant Review*, Vol. 14, No. 5, March 6, 1987 (Fort Worth, TX: Remnant Review).

6   *Facts on File*, March 8, 1985 (New York: Facts on File, Inc.), p. 151.

INDEX

Other books by Hans F. Sennholz:

THE POLITICS OF UNEMPLOYMENT

Why is unemployment so high in the United States? Why will unemployment be going higher in the years to come? Because most people don't understand the politics of unemployment, and they won't read this book.

Here's your opportunity to understand what causes unemployment. Unemployment is a matter of labor cost and productivity. Economic policies designed to benefit workers may actually do the opposite.

To see whether you could be in danger of losing your job because of government policies designed to help you, order your copy of *The Politics of Unemployment* today.

The Politics of Unemployment is a classic in labor economics. If any book can change economic policy and alleviate unemployment, *The Politics of Unemployment* is that book. It is probably the most devastating analysis of popular full-employment doctrine and policy ever penned. No study of labor economics is complete without this book.

Students, professors, businessmen, and anyone else who wants to understand why unemployment is going higher in the years to come, should order their copy today.

AGE OF INFLATION

Age of Inflation is an enlightening and sobering analysis of the history and theory of inflation in the twentieth century. Written from the perspective of the Austrian School, the book recounts the German experience with inflation and price controls from World War I to the end of World War II. It deftly exposes the errors of the monetarists and their faith in political money, and examines the policies and consequences of the Federal Reserve System, offering recommendations for restoring a sound monetary system. *Age of Inflation*, which is also available in Spanish (*Tiempos De Inflación*, Buenos Aires, Argentina), is an invaluable aid to students of economics who seek to understand one of the great evils of our time.

MONEY AND FREEDOM

What makes inflation possible? If you knew the answer to that question, you could eliminate it, right? Right!

Money and Freedom looks beyond rising prices to the root of inflation; it looks to the money that is being inflated. It identifies the laws that give government a monopoly over our money and the power to destroy it. Dr. Sennholz convincingly argues for monetary reform, and calls for the elimination of inflation.

Professor Sennholz also argues that government is occupying an important command post over our lives as long as it remains the money monopolist. He is at his best where he explodes the doctrines of monetarism, the supply-siders, and the advocates of social credit, who would substitute their managed-money schemes for the present schemes. Sennholz's alternative is proven and yet different from any other. *Money and Freedom* is a landmark in the history of monetary thought.

DEATH AND TAXES

Dr. Sennholz's *Death and Taxes* (2nd revised edition) not only presents the economics of taxation, especially estate taxation, but also provides the reader with intelligent advice. When productive capital is forced to seek escape from death duties, there are pernicious effects even before the death occurs. Capital subject to future death duties tends to be reassigned from more productive uses to less productive ones, or perhaps is consumed entirely. Confiscatory estate taxation levied over half a century, according to the author, is imparting a new mentality that prefers conspicuous consumption to labor and thrift. The tax consumes productive capital and lowers labor productivity and wages. Instead of reducing economic inequality, death duties tend to increase the inequalities. This is why owners of productive wealth have a moral obligation to plan their estates to safeguard family wealth.

Other books from Libertarian Press, Inc.:

OMNIPOTENT GOVERNMENT
Ludwig von Mises

Mises' *Omnipotent Government* is not only a history of the fall of Germany, but also a powerful critique of the political, social and economic ideologies that shaped Western history in the last two hundred years. The ordeal of two World Wars, according to Mises, was the inevitable result of ideologies that call upon government for the management of human affairs. People that hail every step toward more government as "progress," and call for more laws, regulations, and their enforcement by courts and police. They are yearning for Caesar. They forget the consequences of total government. *Omnipotent Government* is a potent reminder.

BUREAUCRACY
Ludwig von Mises

In his *Bureaucracy*, which appeared soon after *Omnipotent Government*, Professor von Mises addressed himself to a particular issue: what is the essential difference between bureaucratic management by government and market management in a system based on private ownership of the means of production? Mises does not discuss bureaus or bureaucrats, but inexorable principles of human action. He does not condemn bureaucracy, which is the appropriate technique for the conduct of government agencies such as courts of law, police departments, and the Internal Revenue Service; however, in economic production and distribution, the bureaucratic method is shown to be an abomination that spells universal ruin and disaster.

THE ANTI-CAPITALISTIC MENTALITY
Ludwig von Mises

In *The Anti-Capitalistic Mentality*, Professor Mises searches for the roots and consequences of the common anti-capitalist bias. What makes so many people unhappy in the private property order? It is precisely the fact that it grants to everyone the opportunity to secure maximum income and obtain the most desirable position. In such a system, the failures need a scapegoat. People whose ambitions have not been fully satisfied and whose dreams are not fully realized blame the system. Frustrated intellectuals, writers, and literati become vocal foes of the system.

HUMAN ACTION
Ludwig von Mises

In the opinion of many economists, this is the most powerful statement ever written in defense of individual freedom and private property. Logically reasoned, uncompromising in its conclusions, it makes a cogent case for capitalism. If a single book can repel the onslaught of socialism and communism, *Human Action* is that book.

Establishing the basic premises of individuality and qualitative subjectivity, von Mises refutes the positivistic theories that claim the ability to determine economic events. This premier literary treatise is a venerable monument to the cause of freedom and the free market. A classic in our time, it should be the required textbook of economics in colleges and universities, the favorite suggestion of bookclubs, a popular book in every library.

PLANNING FOR FREEDOM
Ludwig von Mises

Planning for Freedom is a collection of seventeen essays and addresses aimed at the general public, and written as an introduction to Mises' other works. The collection includes such titles as "Middle-of-the-Road Policy Leads to Socialism," "Stones Into Bread, The Keynesian Miracle," "Inflation and Price Control," "Economic Aspects of the Pension Problem," "Profit and Loss," "Economic Teaching at The University," etc. The essays comment upon some of the most burning questions in the great ideological conflicts of our age. Surely, the world is headed toward difficult times, but Mises reassures us that trends can change. They have often changed in the past; they will change again. The current edition includes a brief, but thorough, biographical study of the Austrian School and von Mises' contributions, by his pupil, Murray N. Rothbard, in addition to comments by several notable economic personages on the influence of von Mises in their lives. An excellent introduction to the philosophy of freedom, this volume rings clearly with truth.

Call or write for a free brochure and current prices:

Libertarian Press, Inc.
Spring Mills, PA 16875
(814) 422-8001
Order today with VISA, MasterCard, or American Express.